The Poet's Workshop—and Beyond

By

Terrie Leigh Relf, M.A.

THE POET'S WORKSHOP—AND BEYOND
TERRIE LEIGH RELF

Cover Art: "Working From Home" by Mitchell Davidson Bentley

Cover Design: Atomic Fly Studios

First Printing February 2012

Published by Sam's Dot Publishing, P.O. Box 782, Cedar Rapids, Iowa, 52406-0782 www.samsdotpublishing.com

Author's Notes and Acknowledgements of Gratitude

I am thrilled that this book is now in its second incarnation--and with additional material! That said, I want to thank readers for their support and encouragement, and appreciate the feedback on past articles as well as suggestions for new ones.

This second edition includes over twenty new articles, most of which were published online at Suite101.com. The titles for the Suite101 articles have been revised in keeping with the book's overall style and tone; I've also added a few sentences or made a word change here and there as well. In addition to a few "special request" (and previously unpublished) articles, there are updated exercises, and other surprises.

While some of the new additions may seem redundant, as they discuss topics I have visited before, there are, it is hoped, sufficient additions to spark your interest.

A special thanks goes out to Tyree Campbell, Sam's Dot Publishing's Managing Editor, for his continued support of my work (and yes, for his emails to keep me on task!); Lauren McBride for her article suggestions (i.e., Sijo, Fibonacci, and one-breaths, contrails, and tritails.), providing feedback on the first edition, and sharing her work and publishing successes; Marge Simon, who allowed me to include one of her sijo in a new article on that topic, and who exchanged dialogue with me about the form; Teri Santitoro, who provided additional details to me about the sijo, contrails and tritails, and allowed me to include some of work; Scott Nicolay, who provided material to me about the Fibonacci-no-ku, and allowed me to include his poems in the article; *.mms, who dug through archives, offered commentary and information, as well as one-breaths, contrails, and tritails for the article-in-process, and for introducing me to rhopalics; Ron Sparks, who provided commentary on the one-breath, contrails, and tritails article-in-process; and Francis Alexander, who provided one-breaths and commentary for the one-breath, contrail, and tritails article.

Thank you again, to all the people who assisted me with the first issue. . .I couldn't have done it—or this one—without you!

Just in case you don't have the first edition, I've decided to include the first editions' author note below.

Humbly Yours,
The Boortean Ambassador to Haura
--Terrie Leigh Relf, 3 January 2012

Author's Note and Acknowledgements from First Edition

I don't want to include an entire resume here, but I do want to share how this book came into being and list the "key players" who supported my writing and otherwise encouraged me to keep going. It's difficult to lie out the timeline of all this, as there was a considerable amount of overlap.

I'm not known for my math skills, but I think about 90% of these articles were originally published online. The other 10% were in a variety of print publications and/or previously unpublished. Many of them have been revised from their originals, some with different titles. As the saying goes: "writing is all about revision!"

Back in the early 90s, approximately 1994, John Peterson, former managing editor of *Vision Magazine,* published my second poem (My first was published in a school publication when I was six years old . . .), and my first print articles. Also in the early 90s, I reconnected with John Rippo, Publicist of *The Espresso,* who published a few of my articles, and for whom I now pen "The Mistress of Rhetoric" column. I continued on with *Vision Magazine* after Peterson left, but in general, these articles weren't about writing.

Writer-online.com published my first online column about writing! I want to thank the Knight Brothers and Trish Urlaub, for supporting and encouraging me when I was first venturing into cyberspace. What a universe opened up! When writer-online changed hands, I continued there, and began to write a regular column. Thank you to Mary Anne Donovan et al!

My very first official writing column, "The Poet's Workshop", was published online at writersmonthly.com. Thank you to David Boyne who took a chance on me, despite our rather hysterical—and serendipitous—initial email meeting! After writersmonthly.com closed its cyber doors, Gary Blankenship at *Mindfire—Renewed*, an online literary zine, invited me to move my column there. In addition, I became the editor for *FireWeed, Mindfire—Renewed's* online literary arts newsletter.

Jenna Glatzer of Absolutewrite.com has published reprints of a few of these columns at her website, as have other websites, some of which have escaped me . . .

Since the cyber universe is ironically quite small among like-minded writers, around ten years since I first "met" her, Trish Urlaub contacted me on behalf of herself and co-publicist, Carlos Savourin, with an invitation to be part of *Tales from the Moonlit Path.*

Since the three times—past, present, and future—are one, and time and space can really be folded into an origami universe, this brings me to the late James B. Baker, founder of ProMart Publishing, who called me Moonbeam and invited me to become a ProMartian after "meeting" him through Andree Gendron and Teri Santitoro, when I became a regular at scifaiku.com's email list. Then there's our current "bossman", Tyree Campbell, managing editor of Sam's Dot Publishing (formerly ProMart); webguru, editor, and writer, J. Alan Erwin; editor and writer, L.A. Story Houry; and the Empress of *Champagne Shivers*, Cathy Buburuz. You are all Friends of Boort and galactic holidays have been officially set aside in your names . . .

There are oh-so-many others who deserve my unwavering gratitude. . .I hope you realize who you are.

And yes, I want to thank you, dear reader, without whom this collection wouldn't have meaning . . .

--Terrie Leigh Relf, February 2008

Why write? I may just as well say, why bother to breathe?

Or perhaps it's just a fitting occupation for someone who has all these voices in her head . . .

Preface

I like to define things by what they're not as well as what they are. That said, this is not a handbook in the usual sense of the term. It is not an exhaustive discussion, a theoretical treatise, or a methodical how-to instruction manual. While it may occasionally wax academic, consider that an occupational hazard, as it is my intention that this book be "user friendly". If you want a traditional tome on writing, this is not the book for you. Then again, maybe it is if you're still reading.

If you're wondering how to "use" this book, there really is no one way! Flip through until you find something that intrigues you. Begin at the beginning, but not too far back. Start at the end and work backwards, then forwards again. Repeat as necessary.

This book could also be used in writing workshops, creative writing classrooms, and the Transgalactic University without walls! Please stay-in-touch and let me know how you've used the book, if you have any questions or concerns, or if you have a suggestion for future articles and exercises. There will (hopefully) be a volume III!

I'd like to think that there's something here for everyone—no matter what "kind" of writer you are. Into horror? There's some of that! Into experimental? That, too. Science Fiction? Yup. Speculative fiction? Indeed. Traditional forms? But of course. Personal excursions into your psyche? Isn't it "all"?

Enjoy!

Introduction

One of the fun parts of being a managing editor for what has become a very good small independent publisher [that would be Sam's Dot Publishing—you may have heard of us] is coming across a hot, steamy surprise. [Yes, I have two dogs. Why do you ask?] So here I am, preparing this work for publication, doing layout and other esoteric editor things, with a Doctor Who episode on the telly for background noise ["Blink," if you absolutely must know] and two fingers of Glenlivet on a rock in a crystal glass near the right front corner of the desk and within easy reach [too much detail? Sorry . . .] and I come across the following request in lieu of the Introduction *that was supposed to be here*, to wit: "I'd like you to write this, pretty please, Bossman!" <G>

Oh, dear . . .

See, not counting obscure scientific and technological terms, there are in excess of 80,000 words in the English language. Approximately one-third of these are adjectives. Most of them apply to Terrie Leigh Relf. She is a Chinese onion. You peel off layer after layer, trying to find the real her, and when you get to the center, what do you find? Why, another onion!

Any one of these layers can be her at any given moment. She is at once witty and urbane, suave and cuckoo, agile and klutzy, lush grass and kudzu. It's as if she is playing many roles, and all of them are her.

Eventually you come to realize that all of them *are* her.

Yet she has certain dominant characteristics, and her *modi operandi* remain confined within certain parameters. Suffice it to say her first persona and first love is writing, whether she is doing it or teaching it or talking about it. What you will find in this book, then, is the writer poet facilitator educator Terrie Leigh Relf, Unplugged.

In this handbook, then, as it says on the back cover, Terrie Leigh Relf, M.A., distills years of teaching and writing experience into a coherent yet entertainingly off-beat presentation of how to compose speculative poetry, what to do with it once you have composed it, and how to keep it from decomposing. Each section, from "Ordering Chaos" [with a side of Catastrophe, please, and hold the olives] to "The Kung Fu of Writing," from "Plotting with Playdough" to Unzipping a Rengay, is high on specifics and often includes anecdotal encouragement and examples that drive home the precise point she is making. This handbook contains everything you ever wanted to know about composing poetry, but were afraid to ask.

So there's really no excuse for you not to explore your own possibilities, is there?

And when you succeed, remember who taught you.

Tyree Campbell
Sam's Dot Publishing
2012

Table of Contents

Inspiration 101:

There's a process to writing?

"Decaf?! I don't do decaf!"
—Chris Vannoy, San Diego Poet/Artist

Recipes for Success:
What's cooking in your writing kitchen?

Writing is like cooking. There are many types of cooks—or chefs—and they each approach their creations in a unique fashion with varying degrees of expertise. Some slice their garlic before sautéing it in butter, while others press it to just extract the juice. I've even bore witness to a few chefs who added in the pulp as well. . .Then there's the chefs who love it raw, and will exuberantly peel and toss cloves of garlic into the Cuissanart or blender for divine dishes like pesto. "The more garlic, the better it will be," I've heard more than a few chefs exclaim.

So, the next time you find yourself in front of pen and paper—or computer keyboard—imagine that you're an Iron Chef!

First of all, writing is all about revision. It takes time, focus, and yes, desire. While many experienced writers claim their process is nonlinear, others will say that they revise as they write, moving from the beginning, through the middle, then on to the end. I know writers who revise their work two-to-three times, and others who do so twenty-to-thirty times. On rare occasions, the first draft, with a bit of tweaking here and there, will "work". There's no magic number.

Secondly, glossaries, dictionaries, thesauri, reference books, and online resources are essential tools. Read them daily. Become informed on standard, archaic, and alternate usage. Develop an awareness of the sounds of the words, the feelings, sensations, and thoughts that they invoke.

Third, don't abandon your work-in-process or literally shred it out of existence. (I confess to doing both.) If a poem's not working, put it to the side for a while. If you're in the revision stage, save each draft, label accordingly, then keep revising. Create an "ideas" folder with the bits and pieces. Sometimes, all it takes is a phrase or two to seed a new poem.

Fourth, what is your intention? Who is your audience? What do you want your readers to see, hear, feel, taste, touch, or think? Where do you want to take them? While poetry can be (and often is) about personal expression, catharsis, and all that, the chances are that you still want to share your work with others.

Fifth, you "need" to read the work of other poets, if for no other reason than to see what "other poets" are doing. Who do you like? What is it that you like about their work? What does that work "do" for you? Examine this closely through modeling. Do they use figurative language? Are they conversational? Do they engage in word play through rhyme, assonance or consonance?

Sixth, learn about the poetry craft through reading, discussing and workshopping your poems. Find a mentor. Join on-line lists. Go to poetry readings and slams. Read your own work in public. Writing is a developable skill; although some believe it's a gift bestowed by Calliope (Muse of Epic Song), Euterpe (Muse of Lyric Song), Thalia (Muse of Comedy and Bucolic Poetry) Erato (Muse of Erotic Poetry), or Polyhymnia (Muse of Sacred Song) five of Zeus and Mnemosyne's nine daughters.

Seventh, when you're ready to submit your poems for publication, follow the guidelines to the letter. If you're not familiar with the publication, be sure to read a few issues before you submit. This will save you (and yes, the editors) time and energy. Develop positive relationships with the editors of favorite publications. Careers have been made with the mentorship of a single publication. . .

Finally, what makes a good poem?

In keeping with the cooking metaphor, you could say "it's all about presentation!" Then again, I've eaten food that looked gorgeous on a plate but didn't have much taste. If you're a connoisseur of poetry, you know what you like, right? If you're a "true" connoisseur, then it's likely that you'll want to sample a variety of poetic cuisines.

The important thing is to stay in the kitchen and keep writing. When your work is criticized, listen (unless they're really being nasty, then walk away). Remember it's "just their opinion"—informed or otherwise. When critiquing others, be kind, but honest.

Writing for Our Lives: Passing on the Love of Journal Writing

When I first began journal writing, I was about eight years old. At that time, I mainly recorded my dreams at the urging and supervision of my grandmother, who was an avid journal writer. As I went through puberty, my entries mainly consisted of that proverbial teenage angst, stuff about boys, tiffs with friends at school, problems with family, spiritual and philosophical explorations, and my first attempts at writing poetry and short stories.

When I was about 18, I threw all those journals away. Why? At the time, I remember hoping that it would purge me of my past. I wanted a ceremony, a rite of passage, to transform my "girlish self" into womanhood.

To this day, I still regret dumping kitchen garbage on top of my twenty-to-thirty-plus journals so that I wouldn't be able to salvage them.

Hey—I was only 18, what did I know? It's true what all those adults say: hindsight is one of the best teachers we'll ever have.

Now, I'm one of those oft annoying adults who lectures anyone who'll listen to me on the merits of writing—and more specifically, journal writing. My students are subjected to my rhetoric on a daily basis, as is my daughter. . .I don't worry about my daughter not maintaining the habit, as her godmother gifted her with a journal (and a love of office supplies) before she could even write her name.

She started with scribbles and stickers, "graduated" to copying her name and other words she learned, over and over and over again. As the words became phrases, she still added in stickers and drawings to illustrate what she could and could not write. I also attribute this behavior to her godmother, who would send her letters interspersed with stickers and clip art to represent some of the "bigger" words. I think I enjoyed these as much as she did.

Now, at nine, she is quite well-organized—even secretive—about her various journals. She knows I'll never read her journals unless she offers them to me, but what with her media-enhanced secret agent/spy kid mindset, she continues with her difficult-to-decipher system. She tells me very matter-of-factly, that she has a special secret decoder ring engraved in her brain!

Here are just a few of the journals my daughter maintains:

- School Journal (e.g., based on free-writes, reading, etc.)
- Spy Journal ('nuff said)
- Slumber Party Journal (complete with prompts, games, party ideas, menu items)
- Family Lineage Journal (with photos, drawings, and family anecdotes)
- Fashion Design Journal (complete with mother-daughter designs)

In May, I moved again, and no doubt you're not the least bit surprised that I found a few partially filled journals wedged between some books I hadn't read for awhile. It's now four months later, and these journals have seen quite a bit of action!

I've mainly filled them with ideas for books, poetry, observations, and my daily, weekly, monthly, and yearly goals. I've tried this new technique of folding down each finished page into a triangle so that I'll know how full it is. I'll let you know if this new system works.

Want a peek into my journal?

Hehe...Maybe I'll just follow my daughter's example and keep the contents of my journal to myself...

Looking for Some Ideas?
Why not write about the body?

"Think with the whole body."
--Roshi (1914-1982)
Japanese Zen Buddhist Soto Master

Our bodies, thus our lives, are a rich terrain of natural resources, a sculptural expanse of wondrous contours, textures, sights, sounds, scents, and sensations. What better place to begin writing than with our own bodies—and I'm not just talking about using your fingers and hands!

Why not pull out that old dusty copy of *Gray's Anatomy*! This text has no doubt inspired more than a few horror poems. You could also Google detailed medical sites. My daughter, who is eight, has extremely sensitive skin. Recently, she received a nasty mosquito bite. In the interests of not "grossing you out", I will just say that she has now developed a fascination for the more visceral aspects of infection and the various stages of how wounds heal.

Are you interested in erotica? The how-to of sexual pleasure? Healing and therapeutic massage? Then why not try writing in these areas? I've heard writing with a "special" partner can take relationships to new levels!

Do you talk to yourself? What about to your body? I confess to doing both. Does your shoulder hurt? Ask it what's up? Pose direct questions. Don't be surprised if it talks back—and in great detail. Mine has been yelling at me lately, but that's another story.

Be honest. How many framed photos do you have on the walls, bookshelves or other surfaces? How many boxes of photos do you have? Look at and through these, and then bring their textual bodies to life. It's one of my projects-in-process. Really.

Do you have freckles? If you're like me, even your freckles have freckles. I used to hate mine until a friend told me about playing "connect-the-dots" with them (NOTE: be sure to use washable felt pens and/or ink.). Apparently, some of mine may form the coordinates to my home planet. In some cases, for those hard-to-reach spots, you may need a friend who knows how to draw straight lines, parabolas, and so forth, to assist with this process. Be sure to take a photo, too, and then write about it.

You don't need to be a fine artist to draw a body map. Trace your hands, feet, or entire body. This is another great exercise to do with a partner. (NOTE: Yes, I am noticing a trend with these partner-oriented exercises. Perhaps it's because winter, for many writers, is a time for being indoors even more than usual. Then again, it may be because Valentine's Day is less than a month away!). Once you're finished with the tracing, you can further embellish your two-dimensional body. Label areas with text. Write short blurbs that address your experience with each part of your body. You can also move your discussion to a journal, a poem, an article—even a screenplay.

I haven't traveled many places outside my mind, but no doubt, you have. Do you identify with a particular place? Type of terrain? Beyond the stratosphere, perhaps? What does your body do in these places? How does your body feel when you take these physical journeys? Explore these and other aspects to use as body/mind metaphors, similes, and so forth (e.g., from two of my own poems-in-process: "I am the ocean at high tide, the swirling undertow, the sand shifting beneath your feet"; or, "within my eyes, spiral nebulae/my mind, a stellar nursery").

If you didn't read my column on the Kung Fu of Writing, and even if you did, I can't tell you how much Kung Fu has impacted my writing. One of my favorite adages, often uttered to me by teacher, Jung Shee Rich Robson, is this: "Where your mind goes, your body follows." Where are you going? Where have you been? Where do you want to go?

Taking Stock: Ordered Chaos?

Taking stock. Taking stock. Oh do I ever need to take stock.

I live in a small, one-bedroom cottage with my eight-year-old daughter, who, like me, is a sentimental pack rat.

We also like to make things. Lots of different things, each with their own separate quadrant of supplies. I could fill a garage with the stuff in my home. Just imagine how over-stuffed my mind is.

No doubt yours is overflowing as well.

I see that as a positive, though.

You're probably wondering how I can ever get anything done, or perhaps you're lighting candles or otherwise making offerings to your own inner domestic Goddess just in case She's been feeling neglected. Ok, you may even be considering the possibility that I must have made the Goddess angry, and that like Sisyphus, I'm destined to push that rock called "housework" and/or "home office space maintenance" up the hill until the dawn of a new era.

There's also a possibility, however remote, that I'm a source of amusement for the Powers That Be. Who wouldn't have a good laugh once they'd been inside my habitat? For those of you who have crossed the dragon-filled moat, journeyed through the labyrinthine corridors to my realm, know what I'm talking about. I hear exclamations like: "OHMAGAWD! How can you stand it?!" Or, I have an aunt who's a writer. She lives like this..." Or one of my personal favorites: "what sort of example are you setting for your daughter?"

I'd like to think I'm setting an excellent example. If anything, my daughter and I work the same way. Could it be that she influenced me? I her? Or perhaps we just cohabitate well in the wild.

Being a creative person is risky business—and it's not just the outer terrain of the writer; it's the inner terrain as well.

What risk is that?

The discovery, that despite social conditioning to the contrary, there is order in chaos in the same way that there is chaos in order.

One of my close friends is a Feng Shui consultant. I had the best of intentions...really. Where did all this stuff come from? I need to focus on magnetizing money rather than stuff...

I'm here to tell you—at least from my perspective—that each one of these "piles" are treasure troves burgeoning with ideas for new poems or stories or memoirs. Hey, even articles on how to remove clutter from my habitat, and as it often follows, from my mind. Just as I am influenced by my environment, so, too, my environment is influenced by me.

I often remind myself that I create my universe. I think I'm co-existing in several at the moment.

What are you creating? What is it that you want to create?

Here are a few ideas...

1. Photos. Do you have boxes of them like I do? Well, they can be sorted and catalogued. Or, you could make framed collages—with text. First of all, spread a few piles all over the dining room table, kitchen counter, or bedroom rug. Wallow in them... Toss out the duplicates and the shots you don't like—but pay particular attention to those unidentifiable images. They are oh-so-intriguing, and may inspire you to ask the proverbial, "what if?" questions. Make collages with them, too.
2. Another idea to work with photos is to pull out significant ones and write about them. Perhaps it's a family scene at

last year's holiday season. Or maybe it's of your garden in full-bloom. An urban setting? A quirky "candid-camera" shot of friends at a local pub? You could pull together a series of these for an exhibit—even if that exhibit never leaves a friend or family's house.

3. Those bags of fabric, some already cut out for quilts? Start sewing them together. Add text. Create a story with fabric. Haven't you wanted to get started on those hand-made books of poetry? You could also make quilted or appliquéd book covers.
4. Donation bags are good. I actually have a donation box sitting on my front porch. As I attempt to work through various piles (and oh yes, the closets), I put in things we've outgrown, stuff we don't use, or yes, don't need. This relates to writing files as well. While I am a definite proponent of saving notes, character studies, and those stories-in-process for an undefined future, sometimes that future is the present reality of the circular file, the shredder, or the fire.
5. Speaking of fire...A ritual that I often perform at this time of year in particular, is to write down what I want to let go of on a piece of paper, then give it to the flame. I also write down what I want to create in my life. My daughter loves this ritual, which we did together for the first time last year. Afterwards, we wrote in our respective journals for awhile. It was a wonderful mother-daughter bonding experience, and an excellent way to teach kids the power of journaling.
6. Then there's the list poem—or the list story. Look around where you're sitting right now. Make a list of what you see, hear, taste, touch, feel, think, etc. Each item on that list is organic.
7. Remember to gather and share with like—and especially with divergent—minded individuals. It keeps life interesting.
8. Remember to nurture yourself with time alone.
9. I have this thing for odd-numbered lists, so this is where you can add in your own thoughts and ideas!

The Kung Fu of Writing: How to Situate Yourself in a Daily Practice and Work Toward that Black Belt!

I've been telling Jung Shee Rich Robson of the Kung Fu Academy that I wanted to write a piece on the Kung Fu of writing. What does Kung Fu have to do with writing, you ask?

Loosely translated, "Kung Fu" means "hard work over a long period of time."

See the connection?

In order to develop, you need to have a daily practice. A rigorous daily practice. Ok, so I'm a better writer than I am a Kung Fu student (with apologies to my teacher…), but the desire is there. That's step one. You have to want it. You have to need it. You have to start twitching if you're not getting to pound into that rock bag or keyboard. You're given to irrational outbursts in public if you're not throwing someone to the ground or some character into conflict and resolution.

You crawl into Kung Fu (or to your puter chair) whining and complaining. After class (or after that two hours of writing), you're kissing the carpet (or your computer screen). You feel better than good. All is right in the Tao. You're primed to take on the next opponent or the next page.

Ultimately, you're really "fighting" yourself, so doesn't it follow that you need to know as many techniques as possible? Doesn't it also follow that you need to be aware of your vulnerable areas as well as your strengths? How do you counter a "Right Inside Windmill"? What about a scene where a character's life flashes before their eyes?

The good thing about kung fu–and writing–is that there's always something new to learn, a new level to attain.

But how do you start the flow in the first place?

Jung Shee Robson says: "you can't start moving until you first stop moving."

Many yin-yang Kung Fu forms begin with what is called the "natural stance". You stand feet together, knees slightly bent, pelvis tucked, arms at the side, shoulders and head up, and breathe. In writing, our "natural stance" is sitting at the computer, typing away—or at a cool café, double mocha, pen and notebook in hand.

Some people resist routines. The thought of a daily anything is "bor-ing!"

It doesn't have to be that way. As I've said before, belief is an extraordinary power. Or as Jung Shee Robson says, "just do it!"

Kung Fu teaches us how to move naturally, as the body was intended; so, too, does writing. Since I am a definite believer in the body-mind connection, it's important to emphasize that we can adopt a natural posture when we write. It's not only about sitting up straight with our head up, shoulders back, and chest open, it's also being mindful. Jung Shee often says: "wherever the mind goes, the ch'i follows."

Yes, words are all around us. They permeate all things—just like ch'i. There's a Buddhist adage that I often repeat to myself: "out of formlessness, comes form; out of form, comes formlessness". They're in the very air you breathe. So don't block them–absorb them!

It feels good to write, good to practice Kung Fu…

Don't try to do it all at once. That can lead to over-whelm…Take it one day at a time. Breathe. Create a space that welcomes a writing process, rather than one that thwarts it. In other words, get out of your own way! Step aside and watch how that "inner editor" is catapulted into thick air…

As My Friend, the Feng Shui Consultant, Sada Anand Khaur Khalsa, asks: Is this what you want to give your vital energy to?

What we focus on grows—why not focus on writing?
Ponder this (to borrow Suzuki Roshi's rhetoric): when you breathe, breathe. When you write, write.

Writers Block? Never!

Ok, so I'm not a very good liar. If you could see my eyes right now, you'd know that I, too, occasionally succumb to the "Midwinter", as well as the "whaddya- mean-spring-isn't-here-yet?" Blues.

Come on. Writers are creative people. Imaginative people. We're "all about" solutions to difficult conflicts, aren't we? We're also excellent mediators, negotiators, and are in possession of a veritable Mary-Poppins-purse-full of tricks and treats.

A wise friend and former co-worker once said, "All you need is a round-to-it." She made one for me, too. Keep reading, and you'll learn how to make your own!

We could get all-psychoanalytical and say that writers block is "just" a delusion, or perhaps a sign of procrastination. We could also say that writers block is a specific reactionary device to ensure that we take a break from "being in the zone" for countless hours without sleep, proper nourishment, or fresh air.

There may even be one or two writers out there who believe writers block is a message—and punishment—from The Muse. You've sacrificed your social life and trips to the mall, made offerings of chocolate and espresso—even star gazer lilies—and she hasn't so much as dictated a whispered line in your ear.

It's no secret that I have a controversial relationship with my muse. A friend in a writing group even went so far as to say that I needed to find a new one. Needless to say, I've composed quite a few poems about poems, also known as Ars Poetica, in an attempt to create some kind of flow.

My first published collection of poems, *Lap Danced by the Muse*, has several poems that express how upset I've been with my muse. She plays games with me, ok? Toys with my affections.

And we all know how unnerving that can be!

So, if you've got da Blues, why not write about it. That should get you unstuck. In the rhetoric of Gertrude Stein: writing is writing is writing. . .

Or try these exercises:

1. Buy some of those children's wooden blocks in bright colors. Stack them by color, topple them over—or build something with them.

2. Get a piece of wood, paint—or otherwise decorate—it. In your nicest printing, inscribe "writers block" on it, place it on your desk. Isn't it beautiful?

3. If you're more inclined toward visualization exercises, imagine your writer's block is an ice cube. Take it outside into the sun or melt it in boiling water. (NOTE: You can actually do this with a "real" ice cube if it assists your process.)

4. Get out that jigsaw and cut a round piece of wood. Drill a hole in the center. This is a round-to-it like the one my friend, Janeen made me. Make a stack of them, and give them to all your writer friends who claim to suffer from writers block or the Midwinter Blues, or the I can't-believe-it's-not-spring-yet Blues.

Until next time, remember this: You know you want to write. You're compelled to write. You really want to right. Writing is like breathing to you. You love to breathe. You need to breathe. You need to write…

Adopt "Beginner's Mind" when Writing

"In the beginner's mind there are many possibilities, in the expert's there are few."

—Suzuki Roshi, *Zen Mind, Beginner's Mind*

Whether you're a "new" or a more experienced writer—even a so-called "expert writer", you've probably made more than a few New Year's resolutions that relate to writing. These short and long-term goals may include the following: a renewed daily writing regimen; facilitating a regular weekend writing bash; creating a workshop series; attending a writing conference (e.g., such as the Southern California Writers Conference http://www.writersconference.com); attending a series of readings or open mics; or spending more time in cafes with intriguing people.

Perhaps you're already meeting your daily goals, and want to push the margins further. Sometimes these goals are more reasonable than others. For example, writing a novel in a month is reasonable when you have the assistance of Chris Baty and the NaNoWriMo to support your efforts (http://www.nanowrimo.org/). Revising it with what's left of your vacation may not be as reasonable…

As writers, we are dedicated. Sometimes, however, even the proverbial "best of us" procrastinate and/or listen a bit to that inner editor (AKA ego) who is occasionally in a bad mood. One moment our supposed "friend" tells us we're sure to win the Pulitzer, while less than five minutes later it informs us (cackling like a demon, of course), that we might as well spend our time combing the administrative assistant want ads.

Of course there are long stretches of time when we're "in the zone". Isn't that a wondrous feeling? While some writers are in that zone the moment they start typing or writing on their yellow legal pads, others have difficulty getting started.

Have you considered the possibility that each moment we write is an opportunity to begin anew? We can just "be there" with the computer screen, the legal pad and pen, allow our minds to flow onto the page. We don't have to sit with preconceived notions, undue pressure, or the many voices of our internal editor's coaching to tell us what to do, how to be, and so forth. It's an opportunity to effortlessly expand our awareness through observing the mind "as it is" in that moment. It is also an opportunity to approach a story with the "what-if's", to reconnect with that wide-eyed curiosity that may have inspired us to write in the first place.

When you adopt the attitude of beginner's mind, you are more open, aren't you? It's exciting, isn't it, to invite a fresh approach, a new way of visioning—or re-visioning an existing or new project?

This is not to say that we shouldn't have writing goals. It's to say that maybe we're holding our body/mind too tight by attempting to plot that entire novel before we begin to write it. When we work everything out ahead of time, is there still space for surprises, for an auspicious coincidence, for serendipity? Chris Baty, the NaNoWriMo camp leader, says it clearly in the title of his book: *No Plot, No Problem.*

Go ahead...do it now. Every moment or every day is an opportunity to welcome and experience beginner's mind. Sit down and just write without worrying about where the novel or story or poem or article is going.

Enjoy the process—and yes, you do get to revise!

How do you like your writing?

I like mine fresh-squeezed. You know, like orange juice. I also like it in the morning—especially before the sun comes out and before I even get to sleep.

After I get some sleep, I need to put pen to paper-or fingers to computer keyboard—in order to wake up again. Maybe it's a lifetime of what my mother always termed "burning both ends of the candle", but I've always had an inner-time clock that ran counter-clockwise.

No matter what time it is, beginning my day this way is one of my habitual patterns. It brings structure and routine to my life. I don't see it as a chore. It's a lifestyle, a way of being, a way of inter—and inner—acting with the world.

Okay-okay! Maybe I am obsessed, but I'm still able to function in the proverbial outside world more or less. Teaching English at a local community college gets me out of the house; otherwise, I would probably write the better part of every day.

I've spoken to several writer friends over the last few months who for one reason or another, have difficulty establishing—or re-establishing—a regular writing regimen. They're writers. They want to write, need to write, but can't seem to "break" the habit of not writing regularly.

As the cliché goes, old habits are difficult to break. The process of attempting to break them may even work against us sometimes (e.g., all those internal dialogues with the good versus naughty writer/editor within us). Old habits may shatter into a thousand pieces, embed themselves beneath our skin, creep into the soles of our feet, and so forth.

Not too pleasant, is it?

Here's a solution…

Rather than focusing vital energy on the breaking of old habits, why not make a quantum shift to creating new ones instead?

How long does it take to create a new habit?

Mere moments. Decide to do it—and do it. (It's the way of Kung Fu and Jedi Masters alike…)

Trying to do it doesn't cut it. But it's a start. Once you get frustrated at TRYING to create a fresh approach to writing or to develop a writing practice, you'll eventually realize that the only way to establish a writing practice is to engage in writing.

Simple.

Since you're already sitting down at your computer reading this, open a document. (I'll wait while you're doing this…)

Done?

Ok, now try the following…

See! You're writing!

Sit down at a desk (cleared of all detritus), open a word program.

Someone else is already on the computer and it's not your turn yet?

No problem! Have a notebook handy. Several notebooks (and I'm not referring to the computerized one, although that's good to have as well, but then the issues of recharging come up or the power source or…or…or…).

Get a pen. Open the notebook. Start writing.

What to write?

Anything that's on your mind. Or, you could play around with one or more—even all—of the following.

One of the many positive effects of a daily writing practice is that you can start fresh every day—even if you're working on rehashing a script like I am right now…

Figure Enhancement Anyone? A Few Techniques to Hone that Writing Scalpel!

No matter how hard we work out at the computer, some-times we realize that there's a bit more padding than we want in one area and another area that needs a bit of enhancement.

Let's get out our trusty do-it-yourself-home-prose-doctoring kits, hone those figurative writing scalpels, and create a new—or an improved—text! Isn't it nice to know that there are still some forms of surgery that don't require hefty insurance premiums and co-payments—and in most cases, with minimal intervention!

Turn on that overhead lamp, focus the beam on the simile and the metaphor. Yes, there they are. . .Their relative proximity in the textual body makes for easier access, doesn't it? It's also a plus that their functions are inter-related as well, in that they provide an intricate feedback system for meaning.

Let's make the incision…

Similes and metaphors hail from the category of figurative language. Both make use of comparison, with the difference being that a simile usually uses the words, "like" or "as", to denote this comparison, while a metaphor will equate one object with another—as if it **IS** that object, thus imbued with all, or some, of its qualities.

For example, to create a simile, you might write: "Tarn drinks like an ocelot." If Tarn were an ostrich, then this would be a simile. However, if Tarn were an ocelot, then this would not be a simile because you're comparing him to other ocelots that most likely have recognizable and species-specific drinking patterns. Unless, of course, you have a pet ocelot that you've trained to drink out of a champagne flute like a human.

If you wanted to create a metaphor from the above scenario, perhaps you'd write: "My roommate, Brad, is an ocelot." Doesn't that conjure up a need to put "Desperately Seeking New Roommate!" at your local café? Now, if Brad is a member of this endangered cat family, then perhaps you should call The Humane Center or your local zoo. However, if Brad is from the genus homo sapiens and embodies certain ocelot characteristics (e.g., is from Texas, has large spots, can run really fast, likes to climb trees, etc.), then that ad might not be such a bad idea.

How about another set of examples? A few years ago, I attended the Mars Panel at ComicCon, where one of the panelists said that Mars is the next frontier. This is a metaphor comparing the planet Mars with Earth's Old West. While we'll need more efficient means of travel than horses, wagons, and feet, there are definitely more than a few acres of vast open space on Mars. The question remains, however, as to whether or not it is habitable or already inhabited…

An extended metaphor would be one which was sustained throughout a poem. This would be called the "conceit" of the poem. For example: The English teacher scavenged through desk drawers, clawed through old papers, then finding the one she was looking for, licked it clean of ink."

An implied metaphor might resemble the following: "The English teacher smiled, her feral teeth still dripping with fresh blood. 'O+ anyone'?"

Some people don't like it when you mix your metaphors. They like consistency. They like coherence. An example of a mixed metaphor would be something like the following (NOTE: mixed metaphors want to be extended metaphors but they get all confused and tangled up in the process—unless they're intentionally wrought this way.): "Censorship is a bouncing ball on a stormy sea." Why is this a mixed metaphor? For one, balls don't bounce on seas, stormy or otherwise. They usually bounce on floors or concrete. To "fix" this, I might say: "Censorship is a deflated ball", or "censorship is a ship sucked into the Bermuda Triangle."

Many people really like clichés, which are often defined as worn-out, dried-up, oft heard phrases that used to be clever similes and metaphors. You can make them work for you. . .well. . .sometimes. It's great fun to take an old metaphor and give it a few jolts from the paddle. . .Check out the Clichéd Muse section at http://www.sol-magazine.org.

I think it's safe to say (another clichéd saying) that what may be a cliché to one person, or one genre of writer, may not be a cliché to another. This leads to another point that needs to be made, which is that new experiences and new objects necessitate the need for new ways to identify them; hence, the imaginative, and some say, necessary, realm of neologisms.

What can you do to freshen up that language besides a new bag of O+?

Conduct a cliché search in your work. Is there another way to describe something? If two people are kissing and one says, "the earth moved," you could revise it to: "I just felt the universe shift," or, ""'was that a solar flare?" Ok, I could do better, but you get the idea.

Do you have any figurative language in your poem? Would it add to or delete from your poem? Sometimes, less is more. Other times, more is more. But there comes the time when any is too much. If your poem is flat, dare I say, "boring" (I've had people tell me this before...), or someone else says, "nothing's happening here for me", then you may want to consider adding in a metaphor or a simile.

The first two lines of my poem, "the understudy", are a simile: "you slay me/like some creature from a B horror flick. . ." I'm planning to revise and expand this poem, and have been thinking about further Hitchcockian allusions. What if the first line was redrafted as: "I am the shower where the blonde gets it."

Here, I'm re-casting the narrator as a shower. To say that a narrator is a shower, or that I have a poem narrated by an inanimate object, can make for an automatic catapult into metaphor land. Imagine what that film set shower has seen.

I quite like the idea of a shower in confessional mode... Do you have so many metaphors (i.e., mixed metaphors) in your poem that it becomes unclear what you're talking about? Not that poetry needs to have clarity. Concrete images are good, though. Are they symbolic? Does something stand for something else?

Don't forget that aliens love oranges. If someone is juggling oranges in a poem, that juggler is probably an alien, and those oranges are symbols for planets.

Enhance Writing Skill With Sentence Combining – It's NOT Just for Kids!

Sentence combining exercises aren't just for the beginning--or the proverbial "less experienced"-- writer. Experienced writers also engage in this activity when revising.

These types of exercises can be especially beneficial when attempting to determine why a sentence – or a paragraph – isn't working. They can also enhance creativity, aid with problem-solving, and dissolve writers block.

While sentence combining exercise books are available through a variety of academic publishers and sources such as Amazon.com, in general, writers focus on their own sentences. Although exercise books can be a nice diversion – even fun – there is no substitute for developing the ability to hone ones own prose.

There are a variety of ways to approach sentence combining. While some writers will rearrange a sentence in their mind before editing and/or revising it, other writers will remove it from an existing paragraph and rework it separately. While being able to mentally rework a sentence is a definite skill (and often a plus), many writers need to see the sentence on the page in order to untangle or further enhance it. Writing out a troublesome sentence may also assist a writer in getting "unstuck" and moving forward to the next sentence and the next. . .

A typical sentence combining exercise would list several phrases – even complete sentences – from which to compose a single sentence. The seeds for ensuing sentences may also be present. While it is important to know the context – what comes before this sentence, as well as what follows it – for the purposes of this exercise, imagine that it is the beginning of a short story and needs to grab – or hook – the reader.

1. There was a storm
2. Old trees thrashed in the wind
3. It was night and the electricity went off
4. The storm blew out the electricity
5. It began to rain
6. Hail battered the windows
7. The rain blew sideways in the wind
8. I was alone

When approaching an exercise like the above, it is important to determine the subject – or event – at hand. Is it the storm? That the electricity went off? Who is experiencing this storm? Is this a prelude to disaster? To a life-altering event?

It's also important to choose the proverbial "best" adjectives and verbs to describe the scene, to show action, to create suspense, terror, or another mood. What is implied by the words chosen? The words not chosen? What words could be added to provide additional information?

Here are just five possible treatments – or revisions.

1. Trees thrashed in the wind, knocking down electric wires. . .and then it began to rain sideways, followed by hail that battered the windows.
2. Rain came down in torrents the night when the electricity went out, the same night when the old pine tree thrashed outside in the yard until it uprooted and crashed through my bedroom window.
3. I was alone in the dark when the storm began; rain and brittle hail battered, then broke through, my bedroom window.
4. Just before dawn, I awoke to an eerie wind, to the keening of uprooted trees, the cacophony of glass splintering.
5. Yes, there was a storm that night, a storm so vicious that it uprooted the old pine tree in our front yard, but not before ripping out the electric lines, leaving us alone in a dark house with rain and hail battering our windows like an unwanted visitor.

There are dozens of possible ways to revise these sentences.

While this may seem overwhelming to have so many choices, it can also be liberating. It's been said that a writer is never done; they just decide to stop – and move on to the next sentence and the next, until their story is "finished". A writer can always return to what they've written – and that's a definite positive.

Words, Words, Words - How to Exponentially Expand Your Vocabulary

There are a variety of methods for expanding vocabulary, from reading the dictionary and thesaurus to playing scrabble and doing crossword puzzles.

When studying a new language, learners often focus on nouns, or persons, places, and things, as well as action words, or verbs. They also focus on learning words that describe nouns, called adjectives, as well as words that modify verbs, called adverbs.

From there, language learners often focus on idioms, or regional figures of speech, and slang. They begin to collect words and phrases that assist them in their day-to-day lives as well as those which further their personal, educational, and professional goals.

Whether an individual is learning English or is a native speaker furthering their language use, there are several methods that have the potential to increase vocabulary exponentially! What follows are just a few suggestions.

Etymology, The History of Words

Etymology is the study of the origins, or history of, a word's usage through time. Online dictionaries such as dictionary.com, provide free access to a treasure trove of words, their historic and alternate meanings. It's fascinating to learn how word usage changes over time. Consider the word, “fantastic”, for example. According to dictionary.com, there are seven meanings, one of which is defined as: “conceived or appearing as if conceived by an unrestrained imagination; odd and remarkable; bizarre; grotesque:*fantastic rock formations; fantastic designs.*” The word arose circa 1350-1400, and is attributed to Middle English as well as Greek origins: "*fantastik* pertaining to the imaginative faculty and *phantastikós* able to present or show (to the mind).”

Prefixes, Root Words, and Suffixes

Learning prefixes, suffixes, and root words is another vocabulary-expanding activity. A prefix is attached to the front of a root word to modify its meaning. The root word, "moral", for example, relates to standards of behavior, and gives rise to interpretations such as the proverbial "right versus wrong", depending upon an individual's code of ethics. When the prefix, "a", which means "not", is added to the root word, it signifies "not moral."

These word parts can be located in standard collegiate-style dictionaries as well as online at various sites. At Prefixsuffix.com, "English Language Root Search," there are a variety of excellent resources that include a search engine, charts, articles on linguistics, as well as guidelines for creating new words, or neologisms.

Read the Dictionary and Thesaurus

When reading and writing, it's an excellent practice to look up words in an online or print dictionary such as *The Oxford Dictionary* or *The American Heritage Dictionary*, to check their definitions, alternate meaning(s), and spelling(s). Another excellent practice is to refer to a thesaurus, like *Roget's Thesaurus, f*or synonyms, which are words with similar, but not necessarily exact meanings, and antonyms, which are words with opposite meanings.

At Thesaurus.com, which is a similar site to dictionary.com, there are a variety of features as well. Consider how often the word "awesome", which basically means "filled with awe", is used. Try one of these synonyms instead: "alarming", "daunting", "formidable", "impressive", "wondrous", or "zerocool." Be sure to look up their dictionary definitions prior to using them, however, to learn their specific nuances.

Subscribe to Email lists, Newsletters, and Blogs

There are a staggering number of websites, email list groups, newsletters, blogs, and other types of commentary posted and published by a variety of groups and individuals interested in language use and related commentary. Many of these are free, such as *AWAD,* also known as *A. Word. A. Day*, and Anu Garg's nationally-recognized site, Wordsmith.org, which has a newsletter, an anagram generator, and other fun and elucidating features.

Other Word-Building Activities

Maintain a vocabulary journal. Write down the words, their origins, synonyms, antonyms, and sentences. Be sure to also include a bibliographic citation of where you obtained this information so you can return there for more information.

This journal can also include descriptive passages that explain where the word was heard, and in which context. Be sure to refer to Purdue University's THE OWL, an Online Writing Lab that is available to the public that provides excellent material on citing sources and other academic and professional materials.

Word games like Scrabble™, Mad Libs™ or crossword puzzles are also excellent methods to sharpen your mind, develop your vocabulary, and have fun at the same time. Word-association games can be created on-the-spot, too, and can be ice-breakers at social gatherings as well as in the classroom.

Read Something Every Day

It's important to read something every day – and not just for vocabulary development. Reading engages and expands the mind. It provides information as well as entertainment. Furthermore, many readers enjoy discussing and writing about what they read, so it's another way to share insights and connect on a social level.

Reading a variety of texts is an essential component of this process as well. There are millions of texts out there to be read: nonfiction and fiction books; magazines, newspapers, and other periodicals; website blogs and articles; manuals, catalogues, handouts, and flyers; and even buttons, bumper stickers, and T-shirts.

In closing, creating and maintaining a daily practice makes a significant difference. Some experts say that it takes a month to create a new habit, while others argue that it can occur on-the-spot. Expert arguments aside, begin with spending a minimum of twenty minutes of focused time per day and personally evaluate the results.

Work Cited:

"Awesome." Thesaurus.com. 13 Aug. 2010. Web.
"Fantastic." Dictionary.com. 13 Aug. 2010. Web.

Some Thoughts on Odd Numbers and Creative Expression

Odd numbers are a source of fascination for many creative individuals who tend to think outside the proverbial box.

I'm not sure when I first realized a preference for odd numbers over even ones. Odd numbers are the realm of the mystical, the mythical, and the orgasmic peak, while even numbers are boring, linear, easily divisible, and thus banal. Of course we need both to experience balance, and one could not exist without the other. They resolve each other, and each is inherent in the other. While I'm not a mathematician, a physicist, or even good, ironically, with numbers, I am fascinated by them and how they pattern our universe.

Odd Numbers and Music

Consider odd versus even time signatures with music. I love all types of music, but Jazz, The Blues, Modern, and Experimental Music have always been at the top of my list. Dave Brubeck's "Just take five", for example, is in 5/4. While Blues are usually in 4/4, accents, pauses, and techniques associated with The Blues, along with their inherent emotive aspects, save them from being "truly harmonious".

What is harmony to one person, is cacophony to another, though; otherwise, we wouldn't have such musical variety. Don't we all hear, and listen, differently? Don't our moods change, and with them, our musical choices? Then there's how certain music has the power to alter our state-of-mind, to create and hold a certain type and quality of space. Recordings of Tibetan chants can create a peaceful, meditative environment, as can gongs and flute. The Gypsy King's music can often alter my mood from feeling lethargic to wanting to dance--and in a heartbeat!

Odd Numbers and Poetry: Haiku and Scifaiku

While many poetic forms, such as sonnets and villanelles may be composed of an even number of syllables, metric feet, line lengths, and so forth, others, like the English correlative of Japanese haiku, are composed of three lines, with an uneven syllable count of 5-7-5. Haiku, however, does not have to follow this strict syllable count.

Since it's good practice to experiment with different versions of the same poem, and to discipline ourselves with revision exercises, here are a few examples. Consider what happens to the following scifaiku, or haiku with a science and/or speculative fiction slant, when it is revised into different syllable patterns, etc. New word choices are of course necessary in order to further hone the meaning and its resultant effect.

With a 5-7-5 Syllable count:
carbon-based cocktail
with a hint of feral green
terraforming Mars
With a 7-7-5 syllable count:
an indelicate bouquet
bearing hints of feral green
carbon-based cocktail
With a 6-5-3 syllable count:
reverse terraforming
carbon-based cocktails
on the rocks

Which one is "better" or more in keeping with this poet's intentions? Intentions shift with revision, I've realized, and I actually like all three. As to which one has the proverbial best chance of being published, it depends upon the editor.

Odd Numbers and Poetry: The Fibonacci Series

The Fibonacci Series has proved to be a rich resource for poetic forms. The pattern begins with 1, and is created by adding the previous number to the current number (e.g., 1,1,2,3,5,8,13 ad infinitum!) While this series is a combination of both odd and even numbers, the potential patterns are limitless. Take a moment to consider the patterns of nature such as the nautilus shell, the striations of a leaf, or the whirlwind nebula for inspiration.

Here are three versions of the same poem, "an unexpected cause of global warming", beginning with different points on the Fibonacci spiral.

Version 1: The line and syllable pattern for this one is 1,1,2,3,5,8.

an unexpected cause of global warming
it's
all
my fault. . .
an empath
from Europa just
confessed it - due to love for me

Version 2: The line and syllable pattern for this one is 5-8-13-8-5.

an unexpected cause of global warming
"It was all for love,"
confessed the Europan empath.
As arctic ice began to bubble with cauldron heat,
earth's oceans rose to flood the land,
he relived her kiss.

Version 3: This draft called for a title change. It has a reversed line and syllable pattern of 13-8-5-3-2-1.

The Confessions of a Love-sick Terraformer
I know we shouldn't have kissed while I was on duty. . .
Perhaps it was a side effect
of altering earth's
magnetic
poles? No?
Oops. . .

While the above poems may still need some tweaking, it is hoped that this provides an introduction, although brief, into how odd numbers can often assist with poetic "problem solving".

On Writing Poetry

"Pretty is as pretty does. . ."

—Delonto May Kirk Relf

"A poet is as a poet does. . ."

—her granddaughter

Traveling with Poetry

"No matter where you go, there you are."
—Buckaroo Bonzai
from *The Adventures of Buckaroo Bonzai*

When I first began journal writing, I was about eight years old. At that time, I mainly recorded my dreams, at the urging and supervision of my grandmother, who was an avid journal writer. As I went through puberty, my entries mainly consisted of that proverbial teenage angst, stuff about boys, tiffs with friends at school, problems with family, spiritual and philosophical explorations, and my first attempts at poetry and short story writing.

When I was about 18, I threw all those journals away. Why? At the time, I remember hoping that it would purge me of my past. I wanted a ceremony, a rite of passage, to transform my "girlish self" into womanhood.

Hey—I was only 18, what did I know?

In retrospect, of course, I wish I hadn't done that. Why? Because it was my life.

Journal writing can be a way of saving our lives—in more ways than one. It is a record of our thoughts, feelings, experiences, issues, and personal growth. It can also be a record of self-healing.

Last June, I engaged in a bit of "spring cleaning", and came across several journals that had missed the "garbage". I also discovered more recent journals that I'd thought lost when a leaky roof destroyed everything in my garage before I moved to a new place.

These journals are now safe in my writing area, rather than stashed away. I often turn to their pages to read, searching for a poem wanting to be. Since I'm such a visual person, these journals are my "photo" albums...

In one of the journals, there were entries about accidents and surgeries. Another journal was dedicated to a trip I took with my daughter to Washington, D.C.; I'd like to share a few of the poems gleaned from their pages.

The first one was inspired by a conversation I had with my mother and sisters.

This landscape called flesh

"I don't even notice the scars"
my sister peers close
then closer
to my face

"They flow into the
landscape of my flesh"
I tell her
finger the right-angle
on my chin
move on to others
their origin
a series of
mute flashbacks

We talk about surgeries
joke about reconstructing
the body
my body

"how ludicrous!"
I exclaim as
my mother
no longer silent, says
"they're battle scars!"

Yes
I think
Yes

In June, 2002, I went to Washington, D.C., with my daughter, Willow, to visit her goddess mother, Great Auntie Karol (emphasis on the "Great"!). I wrote every day.

If you know me personally, then you're aware that I haven't traveled very much—except in my mind. I believe, though, that visiting new places **within** our mind, gives rise to poetry in the same way as traveling **outside** in the physical realm. Traveling is "all about" movement; it unveils new vistas—period!

Right outside the Washington, D.C. Science Museum is a park where there's a "larger-than-life" bronze sculpture of Einstein. (And yes, I do have photos of the two of us sitting on his lap.)

Waiting to Sit on Einstein's Lap

Somewhat centered in the Milky Way, his
brilliant bronze eyes kind to children and

pigeons, sits Einstein. Stars, some charted,
others, unknown, form clusters around him

(but perhaps some are pigeon poop…). In his
hands, a book open to $e=mc^2$, and history's

luminous future comes to mind as a swarm of
students circle and descend, clamber up his

baggy-trousered legs for a photograph
like so many aphids on a tulip.

Willow definitely demonstrated that she is my daughter with this one, a "found poem" of sorts, based on an overheard conversation.

The Stein Brothers

(to Willow)

They approach Einstein sitting in his garden outside the Science Institute. My daughter asks, "is he related to Frankenstein?" and

her auntie chuckles, exclaims something about the wisdom of children. Together, they talk about the Stein Brothers, Franken

and Ein, how each discovered something important, something of value: that people outside the norm are often excluded, that

what we can't see still exists, while I ponder the human heart, wonder that anyone can feel alone with so many stars.

It's All About Revision!
(or: Whaddya Mean I have to Rewrite it?)

Sometimes I'm in "revision" rather than "start-something-new" mode, so I went traipsing through a field of old columns and discovered a Q&A section that said, "yes—revise me!"

Why am I choosing to discuss my personal process with you? I think it's because as a writing coach/poet/writer, etc., that I come into contact with quite a few less-experienced writers who don't realize that writing doesn't always come easy to those of us who are more experienced. It's also because there just isn't enough talk about the strategies of revision, or what is entailed with revision, or that the first draft rarely cuts it. I'd really like to hear from you all on this—and related—subjects. I'd love to present your comments in a future column! Until then, back to that excellent question.

The original question was this:

> How can someone learn the skills to perform their poetry? When I go to poetry readings, everyone is so skilled at delivering their poems. I want to step up to the mike, but I'm afraid I won't be able to do as well.

What follows is my response—with revisions, of course.

For years, I didn't read in public much. I told people that I was intended for the page. As a staff member of *City Works*, San Diego City College's literary arts journal, I read at these readings here and there, but that was about it. I did go to poetry readings, though—lots of them. I thought, wow, I wish I could take center stage like that. . .I wasn't afraid of getting on stage, but I knew then, as I know now, that being prepared to read in public involves lots of practice, and yes, drama classes don't hurt a bit!

Then, my friend and mentor, Rayn Roberts, "drug me kicking and screaming back to poetry". (Note: This is a line from one of my poems, and something I often remind him of by way of "gee thanks. . .now I'm hooked.)

My poetry took a major shift when I decided to read in public more. Rayn gave me my first feature at a San Diego Book Store and café, formerly known as The Book Garden. I don't think I did all that well, even though I did practice. Most of my poems would have been better left on the page. After that, though, I started reading on a weekly basis at the Lestat's reading that Rayn also hosted. Since then, it's been a bit of a blur. I wish I'd kept track of how many times I've read in public. There's that resume thing again.

So yes, it does become more familiar, and yes, easier. You may even become an emcee yourself, which is what happened to me.

I hosted the 4th Sunday Reading at Santos Café for two years until the City closed the café in December, 2004. It was a great, laid-back venue, with experienced as well as new poets reading. We had an occasional visiting poet as well. As the host, I encouraged many first-time poets to read in public. My mission, if you will, was to co-create a space (With much gratitude to Robbin and Mark Donahue, who first hired me, and then to Ron and Jill Beggeman, who, by the way, now own Kensington Coffee on Adams Ave., if you're in the neighborhood.) where new and experienced poets could both read. I wanted it to be comfortable and supportive. As with most artistic groups, the local poetry scene had its conflicts, and several venues were considered to be too conflicted, too exclusive, or just downright uninviting. I didn't want that…What I did want was for people who came through those doors to coffee-up, have a good time, get inspired, inspire others, obtain feedback on their work, try out new poems—and the list goes on.

From what I heard, I succeeded, but I didn't do it alone. It was really all about the people who came together for these readings. That's why one of my own personal edicts is that if you don't feel welcome, feel comfortable, and so forth, don't go there!

More specifically, though, here are a few tips that I've collected over the years (in non-hierarchical order):

- Attend readings and observe how other poets read;
- Practice reading your poems—and record yourself;
- Experiment with different types of reading styles;
- Take speech and/or acting classes;
- Read your favorite poets aloud;
- Label negative thoughts "thinking"—you CAN do it!;
- Video tape yourself reading from the comfort of your home;
- Visualize yourself up there reading. . .hear the applause!;
- Start off by reading to friends who support you, then move up to reading in front of an open mic audience;
- Remind yourself of how much you love to write poetry, and that sharing your work with others is a great gift!

How To Get a Poem Started When You're Out of Fuel

I've had a bad case of the flu. My brain is all squishy. I was abducted by earthlings, taken to an underground lab and experimented on. Oh—the horrors! The Horror! THE HORROR!

Ideas for poems? Maybe. But they're primarily reasons (okay, excuses…) as to why this column is so much shorter than usual. Short is good sometimes, right?

Without further preamble, how do you get a poem to start?

First you have to plug it in…

I know the above sounds like it came from a litany of grade school jokes, but there's something to it, don't you think?

How **DO** you get a poem started?

I've had a number of people ask me this question lately, and I've responded with variations of the following: "well, you know I don't drive"; "pretend you're five"; and "make a list of stuff, then say something about it."

It got me thinking, and I realized I've never written a column about how to get a poem started.

There have been more than a few occasions when I've had time to write, wanted to write, but nothing in my "poetry-in-process" files appealed to me.

This isn't the same as writer's block. In fact, the next time someone wants to hand you a writer's block, give it right back—or pass it on. True, you can build things with these blocks, but sometimes the shapes aren't quite right, and they don't fit with the other ones you have lying around. What's up with this "modular is better" attitude anyway? I say mess it up a bit…(it could be the fever talking, though.)

Poems are about action. Think back to the earlier question, "how do you get a poem to start?" Does this imply that it's something separate from we, the poet? That it's a machine that needs action on our part to work? If it's not plugged in, or if it doesn't have batteries, then it won't work? Where's the poem's power source? That's the important part. It's got to have juice to go, right?

There are a variety of power sources for poems: the poet, the reader, the context of the poem, the feelings surrounding—and filling—the poem.

The power of a poem can grow—can surge—when it's fed the right kind of energy. This comes from our participation in its process, in sharing the poem with others, and with sparking that poetic energy in others.

Poems can drive, fly, walk, skip, dance, cavort, soar, spin, whirl, dive, swim, flounder, splash about, and they can also lie very still, so very still, so very quiet, that they may in fact appear dead…or in a coma…or perhaps, fast, fast asleep.

Poems can wake-up. Shout. Scream. Prance and stomp. They can ponder deliciousness. They can discover something stupendous. They can bury something secretively by the full moon on a dark night. Poems can do whatever they want. They are free, free, free to be whatever they want to, need to, choose to, be.

They are little rascals, too. Given to mischievous deeds in the middle of the night or the wee hours at the edge of sleep. They can mis-match socks and shoe laces just as well as spices and herbs.

What to do to get a poem started? Try a few of these:

1. Let the poem lead you into a room with your eyes closed—no peeking in this game of trust!;

2. Cut out words that you like and put them in a special bag, then draw these words and see what arises;

3. Body talk—what do your toes want to say? Your fingers? What about your belly button and your brain? Get your body parts talking;

4. Are you hungry? Me, too! What would you like to eat—and why?;

5. What's on TV? Create a poetic commentary—or parody—of annoying shows, commercials, etc.;

6. Collect first lines—of letters, emails, notices, poems, articles, books, etc., then play around with the other-this is called a "cento" poem;

7. Play the sensory game: What do I see? What do I hear? What do I taste? What do I smell? What do I feel? What do I think? What do I emote? What do I intuit?;

8. Go some place, take notes about the place. Where did you go, what did you do, who did you do it with, and so forth;

9. Spend time with someone, then "give" them to poetry; and

10. Create-a-shape poems are fun (NOTE: This is great for you doodlers…).

It's important to have fun, to enjoy the process, to allow yourself to just write without that annoying internal editor …Writing poetry is a process; we need to return to it again and again. Poems are like people; they do have a mind of their own, so don't be surprised when one tells you to sit down and listen for awhile. Poems are also like finger painting with the soul, or spirit realm, so don't be surprised if you receive a visitation from another realm. Poems are more than a bunch of words all scrambled up on a piece of paper, so add cilantro y mucho cariño.

How to Let a Poem Go

"There is no try. There is only do or not do."
—Yoda, Jedi Master

Writing poetry isn't **like** a relationship—it **is** a relationship.

Sometimes we let them go easily because there's another one sitting right next to us and it seems oh-so-much-more appealing. Other times, we wish we could get a restraining order on them because they continue to stalk us even after we've dumped them. Still others haunt us, and no medium, dead or alive, can figure out what message they're trying to communicate.

Have you ever felt afraid of being left all alone without a poem? Once you have a poem-in-process, do you refuse to let it out of your sight to the point where it threatens to leave you if you don't get a grip?

I suppose I could also ask whether you're afraid to be alone with a poem—but that's another column…

I'm here to tell you that it's time to be brave and let that poem go. It's not like you'll never have another poem ever again. When the time comes, the "right" poem will seek you out—or you, it. You'll probably have more insight and be even better prepared to commit to a relationship with a poem. Really.

I don't know why, but some people dump their poems in a hurry and move on to the next one before they've fully processed the significance of their time together. Another behavior I've noticed is that some people need to get angry before they let a poem go. This is not really letting go; it's an aggressive shoving away. They crack disks, shred paper, bang on their desk or table. No doubt you've observed this behavior at some point in some poet.

It's not the poem's fault. Have you noticed that when the finger of blame is pointed that it tends to boomerang?

Since it takes two to have a relationship, there has to be a balance, an even exchange. Communicate with the poem. Ask it what it wants, what it needs. You need to be honest as well.

Tell it what you want, what you need. Together, create a supportive environment so that both you and the poem feel comfortable enough to express your thoughts and feelings.

If that doesn't work, then maybe you both need time alone to process. I can relate…If I don't get time alone I, well, ah-er—maybe I should keep part of myself a mystery…

You could also put that poem—or poems—on a disk and stash that disk somewhere. (Warning: Some poems will do the same to you. In fact, they will take you places you don't want to go, like "milk-soaked liver and onions on a Sunday!") In fact, take all the poems that won't speak to you and/or that elicit angry or depressed emotions (remember: depression is anger turned on oneself) and put them on that same disk. Don't worry if you have more than one of these disks. Once you have them all gathered together, you just might have an epiphany as to why the relationships aren't working. You may see patterns that you didn't notice.

You can also start a new poem. Start several new poems. Try not to think about the other poems. The **old** poems. I know you loved them deeply...But please, please, please don't take them out to fondle, cry or rant over. Move on. Yes.

Just let them go...

In retrospect, you will have learned something from this process. For all those of you who are familiar with my "muse" series, I know what you're thinking...

Let it go!

I'm trying. I'm trying. I'm trying.

This Landscape Called Flesh

Our bodies are a landscape rich with natural resources, an architectural expanse of wondrous contours, textures, and sensations. Where better to begin writing than with our own bodies? We are the journey and the destination. There are so many levels and layers to explore on this lifelong sojourn.

For example, in *Lap Danced by the Muse*, there's the narrator in "It's All In The Canvas" who is standing "naked in front of the full-length mirror" rolling and pressing her folds of flesh (15). Another *Lap Danced* piece, "A Different Desire: Ode To A Muse" (19), the narrator implores the invoked other (i.e., The Muse Herself or a Muse by Proxy) to peel away the layers of skin, "sinew, muscle, bone" and so forth in order to transcend the limits of flesh and basically "mind-meld". "The Art of Feet" is available at Guillermo Bosch's erotica site, *Saucebox*. As the title suggests, this poem regales an integral part of our body (Among other things.).

I'd like to share a few of my poems-in-process. The first one was inspired by a conversation I had with my mother and sisters. It was the inspiration for this column. The "Landscape" series are part of another collection-in-progress.

This landscape called flesh

"I don't even notice the scars," my sister says
peering more closely at my face
"They flow into the landscape of my flesh,"
I tell her, fingering the right-angle on my chin
moving on to several others
their origin a series of muted flashbacks
We talk about surgeries
I joke about reconstructing my body
how ludicrous that would be
My mother
No longer silent, says
"they're battle scars!"
Yes
I think
Yes

Landscape #1

They burrow like grunion
these silvery scars
if you place your ear against
rivulets of flesh
you can hear the ocean

Landscape #2

I stand in
this precipice of flesh
look to where sky
becomes water
to where
grotesque rifts
paralyze

Landscape #3

pain is a jagged rock face
an odd incline
pausing between breaths
it listens for a heart beat
hears nothing
calls out my name
when there is no echo
I climb higher
shrug off my parachute
leap

Here are a few prompts to ponder. I hope they get your synapses firing!

1. Get out that *Gray's Anatomy!* This text has probably inspired more than a few horror poems;

2. Do you have any "pillow books"? Why not compose your own pillow poetry? You could try it with a partner, too;

3. Talk to your body—as a whole and as integral parts;

4. Get out a photo of yourself. Write a poem about it in the third person.

5. Have you ever experienced a prolonged illness, suffered from a disease or medical condition?

6. Do you have freckles? Play connect the dots and see where this star chart takes you!

7. Have you ever created a body map? Trace your hands, feet, or entire body (this is a great exercise to do with a partner). You can draw arrows to various points and regions as well as write directly on them. Make the journey over the entire expanse of your body. Where are you? Where are you going? Where have you been? Where do you want to go?

8. Many people identify with particular geographical locations. Use this as a metaphor for your body/mind experience. (e.g., I am the ocean at high tide, the swirling undertow, the sand shifting beneath your feet…).

9. Try #8 with a city, state, country, planet, galaxy, or other phenomenon (e.g., within my eyes, spiral nebulae/my mind, a stellar nursery).

Some Thoughts on my Relationship with Poetry

"The relationship we have with others is directly proportionate to the relationship we have with ourselves."
—Dr. Chana Frank*

Writing poetry isn't **like** a relationship—it **is** a relationship —with ourselves and others. With ourselves **as** other.

Sometimes, I treat my poems poorly. I ignore their pleas for dialogue. I admit I want them to go away. Why is this? Well, maybe the relationships aren't working out like I thought they would, like my fantasies played out, or like I planned. Every relationship isn't meant to go on indefinitely, is it? It's not like I won't find another one sitting next to me at a local café.

I don't know about you, but poems blow into and out of my life like pollen riding a Santa Ana wind. Other times, they're like hurricanes or blizzards, and if I'm not grabbing onto doorjambs to keep from getting sucked into the maelstrom, I'm shivering beneath the covers of a book, with the hope of generating heat from an idea that will save me from these and other natural disasters.

Ok, I admit it. Sometimes I let my poems go too easily. I toy with them a bit, and if they don't respond appropriately, I ignore and shoo them from my life. Some of these may haunt me, though, and no medium, dead or alive, can figure out what message they're trying to communicate. (Note: Yes, the thought has occurred to me that since I am a medium, I tend to attract disembodied poets, and they, rather than I, are responsible for my poems.)

When I am centered (or more so), I leave them offerings of chocolate and stargazer lilies, lotus oil and vanilla candles to show my gratitude. When I wax existential, I do ponder the possibilities of being utterly poem-less. It's then that I count my blessings (and my credits and my reviews). Then, my thoughts may turn to those times when I've been afraid to be all alone with a poem, because sometimes they take me places I don't want to go. I admit that poets tend to be brave people (some braver than others, of course, but this isn't a competition.) When gathering courage to delve deeper, to be even more vulnerable, I tend to write quite a bit of Ars Poetica, or poetry about itself.

As if that's not challenging in itself. I've learned quite a bit—serendipitously—with this practice that a few well-meaning friends have told me is "avoidance and procrastination".

I've also been know to hide from my poems. I don't need to tell you that it doesn't work. They know all of my hiding places. In the infamously wise words of Buckaroo Bonzai: "No matter where you go, there you are!"

Where do I hide? Oh, the usual places. In other people's poetry. I read and read and read and analyze and analyze and analyze to the point that I pull out my fiction files in frustration!

But that's often a positive move, as I often "transfuse" between poetry and fiction.

Having trust in our poems is having trust in ourselves as poets. It's about being brave enough to let a poem go where it wants to, needs to, go. If we hold it too tight, it may get smothered. If we let it go, it may warp-speed to another galaxy, then reappear as a new constellation around midnight.

It may also pass on to the "great beyond". In its next incarnation, we may not recognize it, but chances are, it will know us.

I like to think that each poem—like each person—is a universe with its own inherent "laws" and lessons. If we pay attention, "all" will be revealed.

*From her Health and Healing course, "Being with Others", that I took at Naropa Institute in the 80's.

On Resurrecting Dead Poems

I was looking through some poem files that I'd begun, but hadn't "finished". I often call this my "haven't-sent-out-to-be-possibly-accepted-or-rejected-yet" file. Since many publications only accept submissions "the old-fashioned way" (remember envelopes and stamps?), I've been trying to get back in the habit.

What did I find but a document graveyard filled with letters and poems to several publications! I slowly pried open the coffin lid for *Dreams of Decadence,* one of DNA's lovely glossies. Whew—did I ever get a whiff! While most were in the final stages of decomposition, there were two that seemed able to withstand reanimation.

So, I dug them up.

They reeked so bad that my eyes teared, but poetry is not for the fainthearted, so I sank my teeth into them.

You, too, can be a grave robber. Read on!

Poem One:

I've started seeing a therapist

she says I'm depressed
perhaps I should make
new friends
join a gym
get out more during the day

sunshine is good for you
she says
vitamin D
you should take more iron
she adds
looking at my pale skin
the bruises

you aren't in an abusive relationship
are you?

no I answer with a sigh
reluctant to confess that
I abuse myself
weary of incessant hunger
rarely sated

perhaps you need a new job
a new apartment
a new outfit?
they're having a sale at Macy's

she smiles
strokes the length of
a gypsy blouse sleeve
only $20
regularly $53

she pauses

waits politely
for a response

we both look at the clock

times up
I think we had a good session
she says

as if time
has any meaning
when you're
dead

Poem Two:

it's not easy being a vampire

like abnormal cells in a Petri dish
we've evolved
it could be worse
Imagine zygotes
flash-frozen

at least I'm not a zombie
my ex-boyfriend was vegan and
when he turned into one it was like
he wasted away to nothing
it was so sad how he'd follow me
to the local cemetery
just hang out
dig for grubs like some skunk
under the bathtub in the winter

After reading and rereading these (and wondering if I should bury them deeper next time, or better yet, cement them into a mausoleum), I decided there was a theme connecting the two.

Vampires with personal problems, AKA "issues". In the first poem, our vamp is depressed, and so she's seeing a therapist who obviously doesn't understand the depth of her boredom and despair.

The therapist's attempts to perk her up via all kinds of human-esque activities are superficial to this vamp. She is bored, too, I would think.

The vamp in the second poem isn't all that thrilled with her life—or is she? She counts her blessings (e.g., at least she's not a flash-frozen zygote or a zombie). Furthermore, she acknowledges that her kind has "evolved"; just what that may mean we don't know. But there is a link to "abnormal cells in a Petri dish", which signifies cell growth gone awry.

So here I am with two nightcrawlers who may or may not be the same female vampire telling different stories to different people. It would be safe to say that in the first one, her audience is human and uninformed. Or perhaps it's an internal monologue. Or perhaps she's hanging at el café de la noche with her vampire friends, sighing over a glass of Private Reserve with the resident vamp, Bettina (Note: Here, I'm transfusing from my novel-in-process).

In the second, the narrator's audience seems to be open-minded, or in some way familiar, with creatures of prey like vampires, zombies, and genetic scientists. Perhaps the audience is one of her own kind. Maybe it's a genetic scientist conducting experiments on abnormal cell activity such as that found in vamps and zombies and such. It, too, could be an internal monologue. On the other hand, since vamps have telepathic powers, she may be "sending" these thoughts to another vamp.

While both poems are in free-verse, there are other differences: in length, in style, and in tone. Playing Frankenstein aside, what parts should I take and attach to which body?

(Several hours later…)

Let's see what's on the slab—it's undead!

My friend, the Vampire

says
I started seeing a therapist
'cause Lance and I are getting
divorced

so I took her to the mall
bought her a few new things
something sassy for the solo
nightcrawler scene

around dusk
we went to el café de la noche
had an espresso with thin slices of lemon
she sucked on the lemon
added a bit of salt
shuddered from the souls
of her feet

I thought it was the salt
but then she said
Lance is eating meat!

Isn't he vegan?
I reached for another slice
of lemon

well, she mumbled between mouthfuls
of salt-drenched lemon
at least I'm not a zombie
I mean like when he was turned
he wasted away to nothing
but he'd still follow me around
whimpering how he was so hot and
could we go to the graveyard
lay our heads against
a moon-burned
stone

oh how he stank!
worse then a grub-digging-skunk
in heat

I just couldn't live like that anymore!

but when he started eating meat
that was it

she chose a larger lemon slice
wedged it in her mouth

over her teeth
growled

between guffaws
I managed to say
but you drink blood

that's different
she tells me
I always use a straw
say please and thank you
before and after each meal

I was raised right you know
she adds to my raised eyebrow
reaches for
sucks on another lemon
says
these are good to curb your urge
for sweets

While the above may still need another transfusion—or maybe a morph into fiction—you can see what I took, what I left out, and what I added. As I've said in previous columns, save all these odds and ends. What may at first seem like a poem in need of last rites, may only need a slight transfusion to survive.

Who knows. . .it may even be immortal.

A Poet Is as a Poet Does

When I was six years old, I had my first poem published in a school district publication:

I had a little dog, and he always liked to play.
One day, he did not—do you know why?
No, not I. Had he run away?

(I still find myself wondering about the origins of this poem, as I didn't have a dog until I was eleven. Okay, I admit it. . .this was early evidence that I'm psychic. My dog, however, did not run away. Childhood fears and all that, perhaps?)

It's not that the Muse deserted me after this, because I have profound memories of hours of journal writing and poetic meanderings. Throughout my teenage years, I religiously submitted my work to this and that publication, and hoarded the rejection letters. I even took creative writing and poetry classes through the Adult Education Program. Family, friends, and teachers told me that I was a good writer, and that I should keep submitting. There's a vague recollection of someone telling me that the more rejection letters I had, the closer I was to getting an acceptance.

Sometime after that, though, I stopped writing poetry, stopped calling myself a poet. I focused on other things—like reading.

Almost thirty years to the date of my first publication, I had my second poem published. I was writing articles for *Vision Magazine,* and my editor said, "You're a poet, aren't you? We need a haiku—or something haiku-esque—for this issue."

I didn't tell him that I hadn't written a poem in about ten years. I "just" wrote it, and he liked it so much he published it.

Since then, I've had close to one hundred poems published, and some of those were sales!

You're probably wondering what happened?

I joined writing groups. Several of them. I subscribed to online lists. I read, reread, and analyzed poetry. I wrote every day, and revised, revised, and revised some more. I submitted to the scrutiny of well-meaning others (and some not so well-meaning). I looked for mentors—and found them. I read my poetry aloud in public, sometimes to laughter and applause, other times to stunned silence.

No, I don't go around telling everyone that I'm a "good" poet. I do, however, tell people that I'm a more "experienced" poet due to the above.

That makes all the difference.

When is a Poem Like a Box of Cereal?
On Titling Poems

While some may consider a title to be like a cereal box label in that it explains what's inside, there are other motivations for including one.

It isn't unusual for a poet to leave their work untitled, but even the word, "untitled", becomes a title in itself. A poem needs a reference for publication, and in the event that a poet chooses to leave their work untitled, the first line is often used.

Why Title a Poem?

The cereal box metaphor aside, there are, without a doubt, more choices for titles than there are individual poems and collections. Some may argue that a title limits the poem, as it may become a barrier to "entering" it. Others may argue that a title expands the poem's scope or offers clues to unraveling its meaning. Still others will claim that there needs to be a way to distinguish one poem from another, even if that is to label them as with some Classical music, *Opus 11 in A minor for Cello and Piano.*

On Titles for Haiku and Related Forms

Traditionally, haiku and other English correlative Japanese minimalist forms of poetry aren't titled. When multiple poets are collaborating on a "leap frog" (i.e., rengay) or other form of multi-player linked poetry, there is usually a title in order to thematically, or otherwise connect, the poems.

Individual writers can compose a solo rengay, where they play leapfrog with themselves. This is seen quite a bit with scifaiku and horrorku sequences; otherwise, they may be read as separate poems rather than part of a whole. This isn't to say that individual poems within the linked set shouldn't be able to stand alone, but that the poet (or editor) has chosen to tie them together in this fashion. A collection of five or six scifaiku about what happens to the crew of a starship when the coffee runs out, might make more sense to a reader (or editor) if it bore a descriptive title such as "Still Missing You While Alone in Space".

On Titles for Poems in General

Creating titles for poems can be both challenging and exhilarating. There are "bridging titles", where the first line of the poem leads into the poem such as this one.

Out there on the wingless hull
time must stand still
as it moves between
the syncopated flash
of red and yellow lights
the interstitial pulse
of motion

Another method is to use a line from the poem. In some cases, this method may prove redundant, but if the line may be interpreted differently depending upon its placement, it can add to, rather than detract from, the poem. In the following case, it provides a humorous and playful tone. Furthermore, it also serves as the refrain, which is another method.

The Bucky Ball Bounce
It's a frantic dance
so don't search for the beat
where your feet are the floor
and the floor are your feet
It's the bucky ball bounce
yeah, the bucky ball bounce

While a poet does not need to reveal who or what their poem is about, or what it means, sometimes, they may want to share their intention. Since interpretation varies, and multiple interpretations are the norm, a poet may still want to convey their intention. In that case, a poem that may seem nonsensical or difficult to figure out, may be more accessible. Consider this linked cinquain by way of example.

Just going to sleep
My mind
plays tricks on me
even though April Fools

has up and gone. But that's okay. . .
as I'm
going
to sleep during
the day so the nightmares
can't get me. . .I'm just going to
sleep. . .just
going
to sleep
until day dreams
a better idea,
until my software's updated
again.

Since it isn't discovered that the poem's narrator is an android (or other form of AI) until the end, the title, "Just going to sleep", may be more meaningful to those acquainted with this subject matter. However, if the narrator's identity was revealed in the title, someone well-versed in this genre might say that it's TMI, or "too much information", that they can figure it out on their own. That the android is malfunctioning, or has been slipped an emoticon chip, was this poet's intention.

Closing Comments

A poem's title may be nothing like a cereal label, as it only provides an introduction to the contents of the box, and nothing about the experience of eating it or whether it meets any daily nutritional requirements. Cereal boxes often contain prizes, however, and this fact is emblazoned on the box in special fonts and magpie-attracting colors. But what if a poem's title fails to grab us and scream, "There's a prize inside!"? Do we leave it on the shelf unopened, try another poem?

Form-filled Poetry

"Out of chaos, form; out of form, chaos."

—adapted from *The Heart Sutra*

Exploring Couplets

Good things often come in pairs. Given the nature of bipolar oppositions such as night/day, heat/cold, in-breath/out-breath, and so forth, one could argue that the universe of our experience is constructed in this way. We cannot have one without the other, and yet it's both, together, that make the world as we know it continue. It's in the contrasts as well as the combinations. It's also a matter of the alchemy of transcendence, of meaning-making, when these oppositional pairs are in juxtaposition. A springboard if you will.

Consider couplets, for example. They are a popular poetic form, and one of my personal favorites. They consist of pairings of two lines, which form a stanza. There aren't, as I can discern, any real limits posed on how many stanzas you can have in a poem. Consider the heroic sagas of our historical past…

According to Lewis Turco's *The New Book of Forms: A Handbook of Poetics* (1986), there are approximately fifteen different types of couplets:

- Alexandrine couplet
- Cyhydedd fer
- Cywydd deuair fyrion
- Cywydd dueair hirion
- Nashers
- Qasida
- Short couplet
- Split couplet
- Elegiacs
- Heroic couplet
- Hudibrastics
- Nasher
- Poulter's measure
- Primer couplet
- Tanka couplet (82)

Unfortunately, there's not enough space in this column to give each one its due, so I encourage you to explore at your leisure, then send them to my attention for consideration in *FireWeed!*

I admit that one of my favorite forms is the open couplet. It's not that I'm too lazy to focus on a specific meter, as I will occasionally write sonnets and other metered forms, but my work tends toward blank verse. When I "hear" a metric pattern emerging from one of my poems, I will follow that to see where it leads; but if I sense redrafting the poem in a specific meter constrains the poem, I will allow it to be what it is. I save these "exercises"—or experiments—for future use.

So soft your lips upon my own
So harsh the moon above

Since most of the poetry I read in public (as opposed to that intended specifically for the page), takes a conversational tone, the meter may shift depending upon my mood and energetic level. When someone else reads my poetry aloud or silently, the reader's internal and/or external voice will provide the meter—or lack thereof. I often ask my friends or students to read my poems aloud. I've learned quite a bit that way. It enables me to listen/hear/think differently. This is the beauty of poetic interpretation. When we allow other poets (as well as lovers of things poetic) to enter our writing process, we step into their universe of interpretation, into their realm of meaning-making.

My friend, the Diva

drapes herself in Tahitian sarongs
gives voice to French and Italian

women who once threatened
to leap off bridges for

unrequited love but it is the fresh
mango of her lips that lure

the audience close then closer
to feel the aria sigh

If you like the traditional forms of metered poetry, you can give it a spin. One of my oft-uttered adages hails from one of my favorite English/Creative Writing teachers, Ms. Liz Frank-Green, who said: "You have to learn the rules before you break them." I often break rules I didn't know existed, and as another saying goes: there's probably a rule for everything. The beauty of contemporary poetry, though, is that "everything goes".

Live from Jupiter

Radio signals we've been
beaming from Jupiter

to Terrans our voices
cacophonous? Off-key?

We've had no responses—
nothing intelligible—

what could have happened—
NASA abandoned? SETI?

It's not that I have anything against standard meter and rhyme. I've written my fair share. I tend toward assonance and indirect rhyme, more so than perfect, or exact, rhyme. I think it's because I like to be more free form, or perhaps it's because my work seems to flow that way, and efforts to recast it otherwise, often feel more like a dam than a bridge.

the one you abandoned

embraces the unseen
as visible, knows that

love is born of shadow and
only darkness unveils

our true feelings as
she slips into language

abandoned for ancient
tongue of touch

Open couplets also contain *enjambment*, which essentially means that there is no standard punctuation and one line leads down to, or may be "completed", in the next line. Many poems are "heavy on" the enjambment, which can invoke a variety of states-of-mind. I've run into the term, "smooshed together", quite a bit lately, and I have to agree, academic drivel aside, that this is often a more apt term! When words are compacted on the page (or within a series of couplets), expansion soon follows. It's the pressure cooker, or chaos theory, dynamic of contract-expand/order-chaos, so much like breathing.

tomorrow
I will walk outside

inhale the brilliant orange
of Morning Glories

until then
the rain

how it tumbles
down

Other open couplets may have so much space contained within and surrounding them, that they're like the Japanese Ox paintings. When we allow ourselves to "just be", the mind will eventually grow still and thus awareness is expanded.

on the porch
a mikan* tree

its once lush
leaves

burned
by the sun

*Japanese tangerine

If you like minimalism, you may be interested in the zip. John Carley (UK) invented this English language haiku correlative. Like haiku, they are deceptively simple...One of the unique aspects of this poetic form is that there is a set number of fifteen syllables with two distinct caesura. The spacing is also very specific.

crimson flash　　　of neon lights
two-for-one　　　at the Zombie Lounge

How to Write Zips and Zip Rengays

Several years ago, I had the opportunity to study the zip form with John Carley (UK), who created it as an English correlative to the haiku. After I'd splashed about in the pond a bit, Carley invited me to participate in a rengay, where we took turns adding verses a la leapfrog. At the time, this reminded me of the games of "leapfrog" I learned to play with such veteran scifaikujin as Teri Santitoro, Andree Gendron, Andrea Gradidge, and Vicki Tarrani, all of whom I met at Tom Brinck's scifaiku list. This is similar to, but not the same as, the thematic offerings we post on the list.

Writing zips is like supping on tasty flies...Composing a collaborative—or solo—collection is equally delicious. If you love to write scifaiku, then zips are for you. While they have more stringent composition rules than do scifaiku, I don't feel they're in the least restrictive. On the contrary, they allow me to further stretch my imagination. Furthermore, I often "transfuse" between scifaiku and zips just as I do with other forms.

Before we can write a rengay, though, we need to have a sense of what a zip is.

First, I'll show you how I morphed one of my scifaikus into a zip. Here's the scifaiku:

genetic chess—
king to queen
stalemate

As you know, scifaiku are usually drafted in three lines with no particular limitations on syllable count as long as they are not excessive (i.e., approximately 14-17 syllables). The above scifaiku has nine syllables. Not only must a zip have 15 syllables, but it must also be arranged in two lines, with an obvious caesura on each line (note: this is often difficult to tab, so please excuse mine).

During the revision process, the possibility exists that the entire essence—or story—of the poem will be altered. I often agonize about maintaining the original intent, but usually wise-up and let go. As I often say, poems have a mind of their own…

In this case, however, the essence of the scifaiku is not altered. If anything, I've added the obvious.

determining their fate   genetic chess
          Queen to King   stale mate

Here's another scifaiku where the zip revision shifts. Another aspect of this form that I particularly like is how they're often meant to be read across as well as down, hence the special formatting.

Scifaiku:

one last look
before their voyage
Boortean pond reader

Zip:

left behind   on earth
the Boortean ambassador   in disguise

With zip rengays, there are alternating "stanzas". The first stanza is a regular zip, but the next is only one line—like the "one-breath" in haiku and scifaiku.

While scifaiku one-breaths have various line lengths and only one caesura, a zip one-breath has 11 syllables and two caesura.

Scifaiku one-breath:

not for sale at any price—stasis dreams

Zip one-breath:

not for sale   at any price   her stasis dreams

After you develop some familiarity with the 15-syllable zips and the 11-syllable zip one-breaths, you can invite a few friends to compose a zip rengay or write one solo, as I did below.

According to John Carley, "[t]he Rengay normally takes six verses. A solo one typically will go long/short/long/short/long/ short and the two voice will go long/short/long/long/short/long. This latter arrangement is because the writers alternate, and it avoids one taking all long and the other, all short."

so many stars

memories of those who died
just wisps outside the port window

word games with the intel droid vowels missing

beams of light pierce a magnetic haze
that star seems familiar

the air no longer stale first mikan blossoms

Atlantis? Alpha Centauri?
all that matters is she's home

magnetic pulse gear engaged sound of splashing

*Mikan are Japanese tangerines

In closing, I'd like to encourage you to explore this form—and to visit John Carley's Zip School of Haiku and Renku at http://www.villarana.freeserve.co.uk/zipschool/index.htm

How to Write a Pantoum

The **"pantun"** is a Malaysian poetic form that was introduced to the West by French novelist, essayist, and poet, **Victor Hugo** (1802-1885), hence the French spelling, "pantoum". Westerners have taken creative liberties with the Malaysian form, which tends to follow a standard rhyme form of ABAB, where multiple, rather than single subjects, are introduced.

While pantoums can have unlimited stanzas, you might want to begin with a 3-stanza poem until you get the hang of it:

Stanza 1:
Line 1
Line 2
Line 3
Line 4

Stanza 2:
Line 5 (repeat of line 2 in stanza 1)
Line 6 (new line)
Line 7 (repeat of line 4 in stanza 1)
Line 8 (new line)

Stanza 3/Last Stanza (This is the format for the last stanza regardless of how many preceding stanzas there are):
Line 9 (line 2 of the previous stanza)
Line 10 (line 3 of the first stanza)
Line 11 (line 4 of the previous stanza)
Line 12 (line 1 of the first stanza)

I was first introduced to the pantoum a few years back while participating in a UK-based on-line poetry workshop created to celebrate "The Year of the Poet." The Pennine Poetry Works, hosted by poets John Carley and Helen Clare, renewed my interest in poetic forms.

Since then, I've written a few pantoums, and, as a more-experienced poet-friend of mine continues to remind me: "it looks easier than it is." I can attest to that! But please, please, please don't let that deter you from trying this form! Personally, I like the "word puzzle" aspect as well as the challenge of creating lines that "flow". It's fun to see how meaning shifts when you tweak them a bit, too.

While rhyming isn't a "rule" in the western form, if you do like rhymed poetry, the pantoum provides an excellent opportunity to hone those wordsmything skills.

Here's a pantoum of mine—

It's all in the canvas

Naked in front of a full-length mirror,
you roll and press those folds of flesh,
think about Ruben's women, and
how the critics call them art.

You roll and press those folds of flesh,
relishing yet another mocha.
How the critics call them art,
inspires a new perspective.

Relishing yet another mocha,
think about Ruben's women;
inspire a new perspective
naked in front of a full-length mirror.

(Note: See how I used my "poetic license" to omit the "and" in verse 3, line 2 as well as the "s" in "inspires".)

When there's nothing good on TV...
Write a Sestina!

Before multiplex theatres, satellite TV, DVD players, computer software, the club circuit, and shopping malls, people actually gathered together in parlors, sitting rooms, and gardens with their friends to compose and play music and poetry, among other activities.

Originally accompanied by music, the sestina is attributed to a 12th Century French Troubadour by the name of Arnaut Daniel. He is said to have been a mathematician, possessed of a great sense of humor, and a bit on the randy side.

From what I've read about this form, I can't stop thinking about poetry Slams...There is a definite "competitive" quality (traditionally) to the sestina, as it was a form of courtly entertainment (remember they didn't have wide screen TVs or video stores, etc.). Sestinas usually tell a story, hence their historical linkage with the troubadour tradition. The ballade, which often has end rhymes, is a closely related form, but without the "end word" restrictions. I often think of these forms as the precursor to the current concept of the short story.

How to proceed?

Since the first stanza sets the "end words" which are used throughout the poem, work up a few to choose from. You really need to begin with a strong stanza that provides the setting, the characters, the conflict, and the mood or tone. Having a plot in mind, or otherwise having a sense as to where the story is going is helpful, but I tend toward the "writing as discovery" method, as no matter how much I plot and plan, this is usually what works best for me.

It's still in-process, but I've included one of my sestinas by way of example. To demonstrate how the pattern is manipulated, I've left my working letter grid intact. Once again, this insomniac pens another poem about sleep...

Angel of Shadows

A I have been with angels of darkness and of light,
B but it is the Angel of Shadows who loves me.
C He is the shuttle that weaves undying dreams,
D the anodyne that soothes pain-filled sleep,
E the bridge that joins one dimension with the next,
F the gatekeeper of a more bliss-filled world.

F Lured into this mysterious world,
A that emerges between fragmented rays of light,
E I take a step, pause for the next,
B while he waits to gather me
D into a deeper, pearl-gray sleep,
C then binds us with each other's dreams.

C "Yes," he urges me, "yes, embrace these dreams
F where we may create our own special world.
D Without our minds linked thus, in shadowed sleep,
A the Angels of Darkness and of Light
B would steal you away from me,
E then wager who gets you first, then next."

E "If not this night, then perhaps the next,
C we will hold fast to our commingled dreams.
B There is no other way—please trust me!
F Far, far away from this known world,
A there is a spell to stave off blinding light.
D Meet me there, meet me at the edge of sleep."

D And so I toss and turn, refuse to sleep,
E cast runes to reveal what will befall us next,
A open the window, gaze upon the full moon's light,
C beseech the tides to carry me into your dreams!
F I am weary of this wakeful world;
B nothing beckons to or seduces me.

B "Angel of Shadows—don't abandon me
D at the precipice of sleep;
F be my guide to your idyllic world,
E where mysteries' knots are untangled next.
C Is it only within this place of dreams,
A that light is darkness, darkness light?"

B E He breathes into me, and with the next
D C triumphant moment, in sleep, in dreams,
F A we enter a peaceful world, a velvet alchemy of dark and light.

In closing, give this form a try. Just because mine embraces a more gothic tone, doesn't mean that yours has to do so. Modern examples abound…

A Poetry Scavenger Hunt—
Turn those clues and discovered treasures into list poems!

I loved scavenger hunts as a child, and since I believe so much of what we enjoyed as children remains a part of us as adults, I still love to dig about for bits of text, intriguing sounds, colorful people, scintillating scents, and all those other priceless treasures.

Wouldn't it be fun to have a poetry scavenger hunt right now?

Here's your first clue: There's something on the kitchen counter…

My kitchen counters are pilled high at the moment. Here's a partial list:

- Good Luck bamboo plant in a blue ceramic bowl filled with shells, stones and marbles
- Spider Plant in purple ceramic pot
- A box I need to mail to a friend in Korea
- My beading supplies
- Four paper maché tombstones in-process for Halloween and Dia de los Muertos

While I could probably create several poems inspired by the above list, I want to keep looking for the treasure…Maybe there's an even bigger chest of it somewhere else?

Here's your second clue: Look behind you!

I try not to do this often, as my cottage is in need of more than a good fairy with a magic wand. Seriously, though, I take a deep breath, swivel my chair around, and here are just a few things that I discover:

- A wooden beading loom
- A cascading stack of student papers
- A Roget's Thesaurus
- Wrapping paper and ribbons
- Two little green men and their gray flying saucer atop a slab of purple agate
- Origami koalas on a bamboo tree
- My voter handbook

I could start writing a poem now (in fact, my process of selection could be seen as the poet's-mind-in-process), but I need another clue.

The third clue: What is that smell?

While I've been writing, I noticed several distinct smells. I wonder which (if not all) of these will end up being in my poem:

- Espresso
- Fried potatoes with garlic

- Vanilla musk candle
- A bit of dust
- Bergamot and ginger hand lotion
- Clove cigarette smoke

Hmmm...I think there might be a few more clues... The fourth, fifth and sixth clues: what are you feeling/ sensing/thinking?

- It's a bit chilly in here
- I really should turn that kitchen fan off
- Drat—I forgot to call the gas company...I think my thermostat is broken
- Where are those bedroom slippers? My feet are cold...
- I really like that guy...wonder when he'll call again.
- I need to practice my kung fu tonight
- Maybe I'll just curl up with a book and forget grading papers

Look! Here's a seventh and final clue: If you had two or more months of consecutive vacation time, where money and other responsibilities weren't an issue, etc., what would you do?

Wow! Now there's a list...Here's my short version:

- Finish my novels: *The Waters of Nyr, el café de la noche,* and *xenodate*™
- Finish my screenplay, *Unmasked*
- Finish all of my sewing projects
- Bead
- Go through ALL of my daughter's and my stuff, organize, donate, etc.
- Find a new place to live—and move
- Go to all my kung fu sessions
- Organize my photographs into books and make collages

Ok, I love to fantasize...I'd probably need more than three months to do all this...I may as well ask what you'd do if you won millions in the lotto—but hey, it could happen.

Now gather all of your treasures together in a pile. Sort through them. Luxuriate in them. Smell and taste and touch them. Add in pieces of this and that. Then, write a poem—or series of poems!

Here's mine (still-in-process):

I should really go to Kung Fu

but I sit here instead, writing.
Good Luck Bamboo whines: "what's that smell?"
so I turn down the ceiling fan
open a window
light another clove, the vanilla candle

She's been quiet for awhile
but now, the spider plant feels like talking
(she's ignored me for days)
says, "who was that guy you had over last night?
He was better than a tin of that expensive plant food!"
and I say, "shush", you'll wake up Jade Plant.
But Spider goes on and on, her leaves trembling
(or maybe I turned the ceiling fan on high instead of low)
until I pick up one of the gravestones
begin to paint it blue-gray
sponge on a bit of darker blue
indigo
"that better not be for me"
(readjusts her fronds)
then adds, "you haven't watered me in days."

How to Write a Cinquain

You know how I love odd numbers—especially the number five, so what better form to exercise this quirk of mine than the cinquain! For those of you who love, or perhaps, prefer, even numbers, fear not, as the cinquain has these in abundance as well.

If you are unfamiliar with this form, I encourage you to spend some time with the work of Adelaide Crapsey (1878-1914), the poet who is credited with inventing the American cinquain. In "Knowing What Counts: The Cinquain", Deborah Kolodji, an instrumental poet in the cinquain renaissance, states that Crapsey was connected to the 20th century Imagist Movement, and was " influenced by her study of Asian poetry forms and her translations of Japanese haiku"(*SP Quill,* 2005).

In "Structure Brief Madness: Dark Poetry and the American Cinquain", Kolodji defines the form quite succinctly:

> In its simplest dictionary definition, a cinquain is a poem of five lines. Crapsey's cinquain was more specific, a poem of five lines with a specific syllable count of 2-4-6-8-2, usually iambic. The ideal cinquain for Crapsey was one that worked up to a turn or climax, and then fell back. Similar to the "twist" that often occurs in the final couplet of a sonnet, a cinquain's "turn" usually occurs during the final, shorter

> fifth line or immediately before it. Thus, the momentum of a cinquain grows with each subsequent line as another two syllables, usually an iambic foot, is added bringing the poem to a climax at the fourth line, falling back to a two syllable 'punch line'. (*Horror Writer's of America Newsletter*, March 2004)

Fortunately, it was Deborah Kolodji who first introduced me to this deceptively simple poetic form. My first attempts were horrendous, but I've been blessed with some fine mentorship… When Kolodji proposed a cinquain list in 2001, I was eager to join. Since then, I've read, and of course written, quite a few cinquains, many of which are trans-genre, or "genre-crossers". It's not unusual to come across science fiction, speculative fiction, and horror cinquains along with the "mainstream", or the more traditional themes such as those found in haiku and senryu. Poetry, by its very nature, seeks to cross boundaries, don't you think?

I am a definite proponent of online writing communities, and the CinquainPoets yahoogroups e-mail list is an excellent forum. Kolodji states that since 2001, the

> list which has grown to a community of about a hundred writers…I relish the creative energy that flows when several poets work together – and as a result, we've created several variations – mirror cinquains (2 stanzas, 2-4-6-8-2 2-8-6-4-2 syllables), crown cinquains (a cinquain sequence of 5 stanzas), cinquain garlands (a cinquain sequence of six stanzas where one line from each of five stanzas creates the sixth), and reverse cinquains (2-8-6-4-2 syllables). We've also written collaborative cinquain sequences together and created a "cinquain butterfly", which isn't a cinquain at all, but a merged mirror cinquain where one of the middle two syllable lines is dropped, forming a 9 line poem of the count 2-4-6-8-2-8-6-4-2. ("Five Line Journeys")

Just imagine a book-length poem! That's what Kolodji and fourteen other poets co-created! Kolodji states:

> In June, the group published a 212 stanza cinquain sequence called 'May Dazed' through Lulu.Com (http://www.lulu.com/content/131743)/. This book length poem was written by 14 poets over a one month period. Currently, we are planning a Cinquain Anthology with a

selection of "the best" cinquains from our current and former members. ("Five Line Journeys")

Now on to some examples!

Turquoise Thoughts

Hammered
silver bracelet,
desert sky turquoise stone -
city-bound but feels sagebrush in
her soul.

—Deborah P Kolodji

Outside my kitchen window

Above
the neighbor's roof,
just beneath the storm-cleansed,
sky, alongside a crippled palm…
the moon.

—Terrie Leigh Relf

I invite you to submit 3-5 cinquains for consideration in the next issue of *FireWeed!* Choose your own theme and form (i.e., They can be "traditional", mirror, butterfly, and/or linked).

Until next time, here are a few publications and links that I feel will be of interest:

Amaze: The Cinquain Journal
http://www.amaze-cinquain.com/

AHA! Poetry's cinquain page:
http://www.ahapoetry.com/cinqhmpg.htm

http://www.kolodji.com/
The Kolodji Pages:

Also be sure to visit Sam's Dot Publishing, which houses several publications which have published cinquains:
http://www.samsdotpublishing.com

Another publication which has published cinquains is *Astropoetica: Mapping the stars through poetry:*
http://www.astropoetica.com/

Science Fiction/Speculative Ghazals?
But of Course!

Have you heard about the ghazal? Pronounced "guzzle", this traditional Middle Eastern poetic "form" is receiving quite a bit of attention lately. I first learned about this form in my early days at the Pennine Poetry Works listserv. While I was at the Idyllwild Poetry Festival taking a workshop with Richard Garcia, he brought in a few samples, discussed current commentary, and we each wrote one. Given my renewed interest in the form, I was recently appointed the ghazal editor for The Muse Apprentice Guild, M.A.G., for short.

Since science and speculative fiction poets often use and/or modify existing forms to "make them their own", I couldn't resist writing an SF/spec poem for this workshop. Instead of that one, however, I decided to write a new one just for this article.

A Ghazal for my Ionian Lover

"It's time for me to leave. Please come with me, **journey**
to Io?"
"Earth holds nothing for me. I will join you, **journey to Io**."

"I've searched through time and space—no one compares
to you, my love."
How many lovers? I wonder…as we **journey to Io.**

While in stasis, I dream of new adventures, my new home.
He wakes me, says, "it's almost over, this **journey to Io."**

"We will lie together beneath the light of many moons."
Such nuptial feasts! I imagine as we **journey to Io.**

Beneath the surface, within crystal caves, soothing hot
springs.
We refrain from even touching on our **journey to Io.**

We feel Io's gravitational pull, then lose our resolve.
A luscious buffet—limbs and lips as we **journey to Io.**

We no longer speak of Terra, our minds on other things—
Cosmic thrusts, energetic flares—such a **journey to Io!**

Let's backtrack now, and I'll tell you a bit about the form.

Provide a bit of general info: lyrical, non-rhyming, but assonance, line length? Love of a romantic or spiritual nature.

Here are a few tips to get you started:

1. Try a ghazal with a minimum of 5 stanzas. They can be longer, but when I took the workshop with Garcia, he suggested this. You know, too, how I feel about odd numbers!
2. The title address the person to whom the ghazal is written, as with the above: "A ghazal for my alien love".
3. Each stanza can stand alone. Each stanza is related—or connected—by a refrain, as with my "journey to Io". Mine, however, still has a progressing story line that's not usually found in traditional ghazals. Note that this refrain is at the end of both lines in stanza one. After that, it is generally found only at the end of the second line in each stanza.
4. Start with a refrain that consists, usually, of a prepositional phrase (e.g., "enroute to Mars"; "on the Moon"; "journeying through space"; etc.);
5. The author's name—or a variation thereof—is placed in the last stanza, generally in the first line.

What to Do While the Sites are Loading. . .
Write a Sonnet!

Once you've cleaned all the crud out of your keyboard (I did that once or twice...yuch!), then what?

Clean the CRT screen.

Check.

Clean all the other schmooges from the side of the tower and other components.

Check.

Sort, stack and shuffle the cascading piles of paper, business cards, and books.

Check.

Now what?

Why not write a poem! You must have a pen and a napkin or a paper bag handy. Or you might also be one of those resourceful people who still believe in lined paper.

What? You've never composed a poem before? Sure you have. You live and breathe poetry—especially when you're waiting for that %&*($*& site to load.

Overflowing with emotion. That's you.

Call it multi-tasking. As the proverbial saying goes: there's a poem in everything and everything in a poem.

That said, ever since I added memory, upgraded to WINXP, and changed to digital cable, my puter acts like an old lummox. Call a techie, you say? Ah, the techies...Where are they when you need them in the wee hours of the morning when you can't sleep and the sites aren't loading, and...and...and...

Guess what? You can create your own reality with a poem.

Hey— if Willie Shakespeare were alive today, he would definitely be hooked-up to the net, carry a palm pilot in his dusty overcoat, and would be seen dashing about for an outlet to recharge his laptop so he could write a poem or play (or just pretend to write while eavesdropping at a café near you).

But would he do windows? Therein lies the question...

Shakespeare I'm not, but here's a poem I wrote while waiting for a site to load (ok, it took me longer than that, but I started it from pure frustration!)

Rendezvous with a Techie
(with apologies to W.S.)

'Tis egregious the time that I doth wait
for so many sites to load up or down;
my puter is possessed of loathsome traits
upon which the reasonable would frown.

'Tis not oft I behave in such a style,
or feel sore need of a night on the town,
so when he said, "leave it be for awhile"
I considered the possibilities.

Single women want—nay need—quite a bit,
hardware, boot discs, an updated system.
A techie with tools and an awesome wit,
can subdue the most obstinate of them.

While this may be the stuff of fantasy,
make haste through the portal, be my techie!

Triolet? Triolet! Why Not Write Triolets all Day!

While this form of poetry is believed to hail from Medieval France, it is quite prevalent in modern times.

The word, "triolet", means "little trio", and according to various sources such as Dictionary.com's entry from *Encyclopedia Britannica,* the poetic form is so named due to the three major line repetitions.

The triolet is also a close cousin to other forms that utilize repeating lines, set rhyme schemes, and other criteria such as the Rondeau and the Villanelle. While challenging, these forms are worth the time and energy!

Basic Form and Rhyme Scheme

The basic triolet is composed of eight lines, with a rhyme scheme of ABaAabAB. The capital letters represent repeated lines, so line 1, or "A", is repeated in lines 4 and 7, and line 2, or "B", is repeated in line 8. The lower case letters represent the two end-rhyme schemes; however, many poets use their poetic license and may choose imperfect rhymes, or assonance (i.e., words that contain similar sounds) instead of a perfect rhyme scheme (i.e., an exact rhyme).

In order to expand the scope of this deceptively simple style of poetry, it's important to create lines that bear repeating, as well as ones that may be interpreted differently with each passing line.

Triolet Example

Here is a poem-in-process to provide a basic idea of the form. It uses a set number of syllables per line, perfect rhyme, and takes no poetic license.

In a Thrift Shop Dressing Room

She wears ghosts against her skin,
ghosts that writhe within her veins,
whisper she's their long-last kin.
She wears ghosts against her skin,
their mirrored selves, muted, thin,
until her energy wanes. . .
She wears ghosts against her skin,
ghosts that writhe within her veins.

Poetry Resources

There are so many excellent resources for poetry on the web.. Poets.org has poetry by famous and emerging poets as well as articles on poetics and poetic forms. RhymeZone.com's *Rhyming Dictionary and Thesaurus*, while a basic site, is quite helpful as well. Another favorite is Glossary of Poetic Terms from Bob's Byway, A Unique Guide for the Study of Poetry.

Once you're ready to submit your poems, be sure to visit *Preditors & Editors*: *A guide to publishers and writing services for serious writers!* at pred-ed.com, *Ralan's SpecFic & Humor Webstravaganza* at ralan.com, and Sam's Dot Publishing's *At the Dot,* newsletter and market list, and publisher-specific guidelines, at samsdotpublishing.com.

Be sure to read submission guidelines carefully, and pay particular attention to the reading periods so you don't get rejected without being read!

Closing Comments

The triolet is a versatile form that can be expanded into a multi-stanza poem. Horror writers may be particularly drawn to this form as its often lyrical and melodic tones may provide a chilling contrast to an otherwise dark content. Sci-fi, speculative, and other poets of the fantasitc also utilize this form with amazing results.

The Sijo

The Korean sijo (shee-zho) dates back thousands of years, and is still popular today in Korea and elsewhere. It is a form of lyrical poetry, and was traditionally sung with musical accompaniment.

The basic form consists of three lines, each containing 14-16 syllables, with a total of approximately 44-46 syllables. According to Larry Gross' "Welcome to Sijo: Sijoforum Primer #1", there is a line break "approximately in the middle, somewhat like a caesura. . .Each half-line contains 6-9 syllables; the last half of the final line may be shorter than the rest, but should contain to no fewer than 5 syllables."

Furthermore, Gross states that there are "three characteristics that make the sijo unique – its basic structure, musical/rhythmic elements, and the twist." He also indicates that the usual story elements apply to this form, and may be developed according to these simple rules: "[L]ine 1 of the 3-line pattern introduces a situation or problem; line 2 develops or "turns" the idea in a different direction; and line 3 provides climax and closure. Think of the traditional 3-part structure of a narrative (conflict, complication, climax) or the 3-part division of the sonnet, and you'll see the same thing happening."

As with the Tanka, which is a Japanese lyrical form, the sijo is well-situated for genre poets and their respective tropes. While many of the sijo I've read haven't had titles, others have, and I'm assuming, perhaps incorrectly, that similar to tanka, they are not traditionally titled. It appears, however, that collections have titles, as well as thematically-linked poems.

Since I am better acquainted with the tanka, but by no means an expert on the form, the request for this article posed a personal challenge, and one that I definitely relished. What follows are a few of my first attempts with brief commentary and revisions. They are, as you will clearly see, still works-in-process, as they do not fully embody the spirit of sijo.

This first poem is 49 syllables, which exceeds the approximate word count. I've provided the syllable count after each line. I'm not sure if the ellipsis works to denote the caesura, and will probably shift to a comma instead. On the other hand, the ellipsis, which is used to denote a pause, as well as to denote or imply that there is something missing, may work after all.

Beneath the waning moon, I wait. . .dark clouds shrouding your starship.(15)
Please hurry, as it will be dawn soon. . .and the pier will come alive. (15)
A pelican dives, resurfaces. . . I realize you have abandoned me again. (19)

In the following revision, there are 47 syllables. I made some word changes, reoriented the second line, rephrased the third line as a question, and provided alternate punctuation.

Beneath the waning moon, I wait; dark clouds cloaking your starship. (15)
Dawn will be here soon, and the pier will fill with curious fishermen. (17)
A pelican dives, resurfaces. . . have you abandoned me? (15)

The second poem is 43 syllables. It's a mix of science as well as speculative tropes, and contains a bit of a humorous twist.

Just 2,000 or so light years from earth, Kepler-11 awaits us. (18)
Remote viewers travel thoughtspeed, wade through streams of gas, water. (15)
I open the portal, step through, amused. (10)

This third poem has 42 syllables. When I wrote the first and second drafts, there were only infinitives at the ends of lines 1 and 2;

after revising it the 5th or 6th time, however, I decided to end each line accordingly. In some ways, this reminds me of a ghazal. While I do like the title, I'm not sure if it allows for polysemy, or multiple interpretations. While the scientific terms aren't necessarily lyric, the subject to which it refers may be incredibly so: the foreplay—and ensuing consummation--of two aliens in-love (or lust).

The Neurotoxin of Love

Your hair a cluster of neurons, with dendrites reaching.(13)
Just one look into your eyes, my axons writhing. (12)
How your vesicle fuses with my presynaptic membrane, linking. (17)

In the following revision, the syllable count is only 38, the title is integrated into the poem, lines 1 and 2 combined, and the poem's tone is slightly shifted.

Writhing at first touch, dendrites, axons. . . (9)
Energetic transmissions - Ah! The bittersweet neurotoxin of love. . .(18)
Neurons in symphony, lightning cadenza! (11)

I asked my friend, Marge Simon, the editor of *Star*Line,* if she had a sijo I could include in this article. She sent me the untitled one below, a 46-syllable untitled poem comprised of four, rather than three lines. I believe her poem possesses a lyrical quality that is missing in my examples. Furthermore, there is room for polysemy, or multiple interpretations.

I walked upon a moonlit path, a stranger in a twilight land, (11)
where starry satellites are more than blinking memories (14)
what strange force compels me on this lonely route (11)
that I might find another kindred soul (10)

I also asked my friend, Teri Santitoro, the editor of *Scifaikuest,* whether she was open to receiving sijo, and if she had any comments—or poems—to share. *Scifaikuest* does indeed accept sijo, and she offered some commentary as well. The "first half of line three employs a twist by means of a surprise in meaning, sound, tone, or other devise." Furthermore, the poem must end with a surprise. It is also important, she continues, to "avoid choppy lines. Each line and transition should be smooth, no more than two rhymed lines/internal rhyme preferred." In closing, she stated that one "should be able to read the first halves of lines as one poem, and the second half as another."

Writing as xeno-unit, she offered the following three poems by way of example. She broke the three lines in two to demonstrate the pauses.

dreadful midnight encounter
pale, haunting apparition
gaze locks on hypnotic eyes
strength of will seeps slowly away
startled suddenly awake **<THE TWIST>**
heartbeat slows as dreamscape fades

*

odd conversation we had
strangers, trying to connect
differing cultures and languages
I recognized her words
but she sees through Martian eyes **<THE TWIST>**
and I didn't understand

*

silent watchers surveying
twinkling lights far below
regarding thriving metropolis
in frozen stone horror
as their creators destroy **<THE TWIST>**
the gargoyles' foundations

As you can no doubt see, this form lends itself to science and speculative fiction as well as horror tropes. Fantasy will also find a home in this form. While I definitely recommend reading traditional sijo, as well sijo from genre poets experienced with this form, there is absolutely no reason why you can't just start now with the guidelines above. I plan to spend more time with this deceptively simple form. . .

Suggested Market Resources

There are many genre publications that accept minimalistic poetry even if they don't specify a particular form in their guidelines.

Astropoetica: Mapping the stars through poetry, edited and published by Emily Gaskin, is an online publication. Guidelines are available at http://www.astropoetica.com/guidelines.html.

Ralan's SpecFic & Humor Webstravaganza is a veritable treasure trove of listings for publications seeking poetry, among other forms of writing. The site entrance is available at: http://ralan.com.

Sam's Dot Publishing has a number of publications that accept poetry. In addition to *Scifaikust,* a well-written sijo (as long as it fits the guidelines, etc.) could be accepted for *Aoife's Kiss, Hungur, Illumen, ParABnormal Digest, Shelter of Darkbess, Spaceports & Spidersilk, Sounds of the Night, The Fifth Dimension, and/or The Martian Wave.Scifaikuest,* edited by Teri Santitoro, and published by Sam's Dot Publishing, has both an online and print version. Guidelines are available at
http://samsdotpublishing.com/scifaikuestguide.htm.

*Star*Line,* "the official newsletter and network instrument of the SFPA", is edited by Marge Simon. Guidelines are available at http://www.sfpoetry.com/starline.html.

Suggested Resources for information on the sijo

Ahapoetry
http://www.ahapoetry.com/sijo.htm

Sijo Masters in Translation
As its title signifies, this site contains work by. . .in translation.
http://thewordshop.tripod.com/Sijo/masters.html

Sijo Poetry
While this site claims to be under construction, there is already quite a bit of helpful information here.
http://www.sijopoetry.com/

Work Cited:

Gross, Larry. "Sijo Primer." *Sijo Poetry*. Sijopoetry.com, 30 Nov. 2010. Web. 28 April 2011.
Santitoro, Teri. Online interview. 2 May 2011.
Simon, Marge. Online interview. 2 May 2011.

Breathing Exercises for Poets. . . Or How to Write Science and Speculative Fiction One-breaths, Contrails, and Tritails

Inhale. . .exhale. . .repeat as necessary.

Writing poetry is like breathing, and just like breathing, it often occurs involuntarily, and may also cause one to lose, hold, or expel their breath like winter wind.

It may not be surprising to learn that writers of minimalistic poetry often host their own events, as reading short poems creates a certain type of space. While this could be said of all poetry venues, minimalistic poetry is so immediate, that if an audience isn't paying attention, they may miss the poem entirely. Given this dynamic, minimalist poets such as haikujin, often read each poem three times. One of the reasons behind this treatment is that with each reading, the poem is able to settle into the audience's consciousness.

If you've attended readings where most of the poems go beyond a page, a minimalist poet may provide a stark contrast to the other offerings. In general, minimalist poets attending the proverbial "regular" readings will provide a brief introduction to the form in order to prepare the audience.

Depending upon the nature of the poems, whether or not they are part of a thematic series, or read by multiple voices, the energy of this poetic performance space may shift from contemplative to humorous within the span of a breath. In this way, poetry is poetry is poetry.

English-correlative haiku and scifaiku are composed in three lines, with approximately 17 syllables distributed over these lines. One of the general rules is that these may be read within a single breath.

plagues-R-us
one-stop shopping
coming to a galaxy near you

--semi*

(*semi is my scifaikujin name which was bestowed upon me by one of my mentors. It means *cicada* in Japanese.)

The haiku or scifaiku one-breath, however, is situated on a single line, as is traditional Japanese haiku, and contains fewer syllables. For many poets, the juxtaposition of ideas and observations is heightened in this form.

One of the benefits of having a poem on a single line, is that the mind can "inhale" it in a gaze. Breaking it down to three lines, while compact, may disrupt the flow and the manner in which it is interpreted. While I definitely support multiple interpretations, and it would be safe to say that most scifaikujin welcome this as well, and intentionally set up this possibility, there may be cases where it proves problematic.

Haikujin Francis W. Alexander offered several examples of his one-breaths, and said "I try to write one breaths so that I can read them straight through without taking a breath. I like to feel the sensations and experience an emotion as well."

drive by -- ghostly faces glaring back

he itch, then pain -- space earwigs[1]

For the uninitiated, one-breaths may be confused with contrails. I had actually forgotten about the contrail form until this article was requested. After looking through years of notes and files, I came up empty, and so emailed the scifaikulist, and *.mms was kind enough to respond. Apparently, someone on the list had suggested that one of my early poems was a contrail. *.mms sent me the poem, and said that "It's not a contrail, but a lovely one-breath."

pouring starlight into moonlight, then back again...
-semi

---

[1] First published in *Scifaikuest,* February 2006, p. 27.

She then provided additional guidance:

> A contrail is a one-line scifaiku with the syllable count as minimal as possible. It borders on aphorism with an SF or fantasy observation or definition. The link between the two halves is NOT literal; it's an allegory, allusion, analogy or Zen pun. Contrails can be serious or humourous wordplay.

*.mms also provided two of her contrails by way of example:

weed   biodiversity

self denial   no thyself

To further explain the difference between one-breaths and contrails, *.mms stated that

> A one-breath also has two parts on the same line, but the 2nd has a more haiku-like balance/observation/comparison with the first half. These halves generally have a few more syllables, but they should have symmetrical rhythm and/or syllable count if possible. NOT make-or-break, but these are supposed to be poetry. One-breaths can be serious or humourous, too.

the lights on all night: Geiger bath fixtures

return trip unlikely. . .memories past perfect

plumbing its decadence -- civilization

--*.mms

While I haven't consciously penned many contrails over the years, I have composed a number of one-breaths. As a result, I realize that I often tend to blend the sensibility of the one-breath with the contrail. While the rhythm isn't exactly symmetrical, each phrase within the following contrail is exactly seven syllables.

post-coital hibernation - his slick simulated skin

--semi

Teri Santitoro, whose scifaikujin names are Xeno-unit and Sakyu, is the editor for Sam's Dot Publishing's *scifaikuest.* She also responded to my call for comments and examples, and said that a contrail is "Two brief lines, the second making an observation or definition."

spying eyes…view screen on

a stitch in time -- temporal anomaly

top of the world. . . .alien perspective

moving constellations...........star trek

--Xeno-unit

Recently, I came across tritails on the scifaiku list. I'm not sure who created the form, and efforts to determine this have not prevailed. I was definitely struck by how sparse and evocative they were. Furthermore, as I am quite fond of list poems and the reality, speculative or otherwise, that they unveil, I was pleased to note that tritails appeared to encourage this device. While this may reflect that particular poet's mood and/or idea at the time, it does differ from scifaiku, which as a general rule, does not encourage itemization in the same style.

Another aspect of the tritail form which was appealing, and is connected with other minimalistic forms, as well as poetry in general, is juxtaposition, associative thinking, and of course, metaphor and metonymy.

Tritails, as the prefix "tri", reveals, are composed of three units, or phrases. While I am by no means an expert on this form, it appears that syllable counts should be minimal. As to punctuation, I don't see why each unit couldn't be separated by space, but the ones I read on the list used an ellipsis. These two tritails were the first ones that I wrote.

ice cream. . .caffeine. . .stuff from Earth

left alive. . .heightened senses. . .intranet

--semi

I decided to revise them, and while they use more, rather than fewer syllables, I believe the revisions clarify the points I wanted to make.

jamoca almond fudge. . .vanilla lattes. . .stuff I miss from Earth

short circuited. . .heightened senses. . .intra becomes internet

--semi

Since I often revise my work into different forms as an exercise as well as to see if they "work better" in another style, I redrafted the above tritails into "regular" scifaiku. I'm not sure if the above are really tritails if they can be so easily reformatted as scifaiku.

jamoca almond fudge
vanilla lattes
stuff I miss from Earth

short circuited
heightened senses
intra becomes internet

--semi

The following two tritails penned by *.mms, were inspired by elements in the Period Table, included in Ron Spark's *Periodic Table of Haiku*, a project he started at his now deactivated site, *iSciFiStory.com.* It was subsequently published by *Science Magazine* in 2003, was featured on NPR's "All Things Considered".

This one was inspired by the element, Protactinium Pa 91.

needle eye...pitchblended...darkest heart

--*.mms

This one was inspired by Caesium / Cesium Cs 55.

parallel blues -- metronomic fire -- caesium kiss

--*.mms

Enjoy exploring these forms! There's an entire galaxy of resources available, too. Here are just a few to add to your bookmarks.

Tom Brinks *SciFaiku.com* science fiction haiku site, is famous for *The Scifaiku Manifesto,* the scifaiku list, and other excellent resources.
http://www.scifaiku.com/index.html

Jane Reichhold's The *Aha Poetry* site has a wealth of articles, a season word list, and she recently added her free downloadable Bare Bones School of Haiku course. This is an excellent place to begin to learn to compose "traditional" haiku.
http://www.ahapoetry.com/haiku.htm

If you're into cool nerdie-geekie stuff, check out ThinkGeek.com! In addition to accepting techie haiku (of the 5-7-5 variety only), they have poetry magnets and other can't-live-without-it stuff.
http://www.thinkgeek.com/haiku/index.shtml

Works Cited

Santitoro, Teri. "Re: One-breaths, Contrails, and Tritails." Message to Terrie Leigh Relf. 30 May 2011. E-mail.

--. "Re: One-breaths, Contrails, and Tritails." Message to Terrie Leigh Relf. 1 June 2011. E-mail.

Serpento, Mary Margaret. "Re: One-breaths, Contrails, and Tritails." Message to Terrie Leigh Relf. 28 May 2011. E-mail.

--. "Re: One-breaths, Contrails, and Tritails." Message to Terrie Leigh Relf. 29 May 2011. E-mail.

--. "Re: One-breaths, Contrails, and Tritails." Message to Terrie Leigh Relf. 2 June 2011. E-mail.

The Fictional Universe

Truth is stranger than fiction.

—unknown

It's all fiction anyway. . .we make it up as we go along.

—an unnamed character in my story, "For You"

There are three sides to every story. . .my side, your side, and what really happened.

--Walter Cronkite

Plotting with Playdough

Remember the ecstasy of new Play Dough? The possibilities unveiled by opening the lid to golden yellow, vibrant blue, electric red, pristine white, phosphorescent green?

Ah — the scent of artistic promise! Remember how you reached your chubby little hands into the container, submerged your fingers, savored the sensation, then gathered a handful, which you lifted to your nose?

Just you and your Play Dough — no little brothers or sisters or neighbor kids with their grimy, gooey hands touching it, slobbering on it, or mixing the colors.

Go ahead — take it out of the plastic container, smoosh and goosh it around. That's it. Take it nice and slow, revel in it.

You're rolling it into coils — first a snake, then a bowl, now a caterpillar with wings.

Now you're really working it, forming one glob into a body, other globs into arms and legs, and you find you're even mixing the colors — got to have beady little eyes on that monster you're making, right?

What does all this have to do with writing — or plotting — you ask?

Just take this bit away, squish that one in there, borrow from another tub — even the dirty, dried and caked one, because it still has the scent of creativity oozing from its mangled container and cracked lid.

What happens when you take too much away (or get stingy with that unopened container that you're "saving for later")? It can be as overwhelming as that first moment when you opened the lid to the story, or as wondrous as that epiphanic moment when you realized that blue and red make purple.

If you run out of play dough, and you're still building that space station on the far side of the moon, fear not! You can always make more with all the recipes on the web…

You can do it - just visit your local market's kiddie section, reach into the bin, pull out a package of play dough and unveil that wondrous big sky mind of childhood where anything can be — or become — real.

Researching Your Way to Believable Settings: It's in those pesky little details, isn't it?

Creating believable settings sometimes takes research—especially if you don't have direct experience of what you're writing about.

What happened to write what you know?

Exactly. But no one person knows everything, hence the indispensable aspect of research.

Research isn't always difficult or particularly time-consuming, though. True, you could read volumes on history and local color, architecture and the local business scene before you even begin the first draft of your novel. You could also cruise the net, make a few phone calls—or send a few e-mails—in order to access these same volumes. It's not that I don't suggest or encourage reading, but I for one know how it can be an excellent avoidance tactic.

How do we know when it's time to conduct research?

It depends upon what you need or want to know. It can be something simple, like determining which plants thrive there and which may need a greenhouse. Finding out the name and location of a trendy café is often just a click or phone call away. The same holds true with local parks, markets, post offices, and high-rent districts.

That said, what if we're writing a novel set in Seattle, Washington, and we haven't lived there since we were three? Maybe we remember picking berries at grandma's house, or going 'round-and-round in the little boats at the park. Or maybe we remember riding the elephants or how fun it was to trudge through the cold, wet snow in our little red snowsuit. These memories may be "flashshots" in our mind, a collage of experiences without much running narrative; they may also be based on photographs in an album, and what we "remember" arises from these images and the ongoing narrative from family and friends.

While I would like to revisit Seattle, it's not feasible now, so part of my early research involved contacting friends in the area who were more than happy to send me all sorts of links and quite colorful commentary. My parents also shared a story about a restaurant that has found its way into the novel. Several realtors also responded to my queries for information and seemed to really enjoy participating in my madness!

I'm co-authoring a vampire saga with Henry Lewis Sanders currently titled *Blood Journey.* Who knows what major revision this is, but the good news is that now we're laying in more specific details.

For example, our family of vampires wants to travel by ship from London, England, to Seattle, Washington. At first, we gave the ship a name, had them ensconced in a comfortable cabin, and made a note to find out how long it would take to travel from point A to point B. We didn't think this was going to be a big deal, just a minor detail, a matter of a phone call to determine a few details to make the trip believable.

Well, after calling a few travel agencies and cruises lines was I ever surprised! The agents were extremely helpful, by the way. I pretended to be taking the trip with friends with the first one, but with the second, I fessed up, told her I was a writer trying to get her characters from point A to Point B.

Not only did I learn (amidst chuckles and sighs) that this wasn't a very practical trip, but that it would be difficult to do—period. It would take about four months, several different cruise lines, and thousands and thousands of dollars!

I'll be honest. I wanted to get them on a plane as fast as possible. Forget the ship.

After a few minutes of realizing that this was one of those unexpected challenges, I took a deep breath and thought about it.

And thought about it. . .

And thought about it. . .

Without giving too much away, I decided that it could be a short cruise—from London to Boston. A mere twelve days. The cruise trip could be a special treat for one of the vampires, as she missed traveling down the Nile on her barge. After arriving in Boston, they could take in the sights, then take a plane to Seattle.

Whew! I feel like I went on the trip already. . .and I'm not even finished writing about it.

So, the next time you sit down with your novel, look for the details. Readers will forgive a lot if they like the book, but what if one of your biggest fans is a travel agent—or an Egyptian Queen traveling from London to Seattle?

You want to give them the details that they crave!

Come on, Come on, Do the NaNoWriMo With me. . .

I e-mailed a writer friend of mine last week to ask if he was doing the NaNoWriMo.

"I don't know that dance," he replied. "Is it like the Mambo? The Cha-cha?"

"It's not a dance," I tell him, realizing by his ensuing comments that he really didn't know what I was talking about, and was not, therefore, attempting to be funny.

"It's the National Novel Writers Month writing contest," (http://www.nanowrimo.org/) I type in (thinking how these words should really go into my novel count). "We write a 50,000-word novel in a month."

"Do agents read it?"

"No," I tell him, "but it's an opportunity to get a first draft done."

"Whaddya get from this again?"

"A first draft."

"Is it any good?" he asks.

"So far, it (insert expletive of your choice as I won't type in the one I used...)," I say, "but it's a first draft. Proceeds go to building libraries and to raise literacy awareness. It's also a great bonding process if you have a writing partner."

"Oh," he says.

"Oh" is what a lot of my friends and students are saying, looking at me incredulously. Every once in awhile, someone will ask me my word count. Just in case you're wondering, it's at about 25,300 right now, with two weeks, fourteen days, and I don't know how many hours, minutes or seconds to go. Chris Baty over at nanowrimo.org has the countdown posted and regularly updated, if you're interested.

So, on Sunday afternoon when I limped into Rebecca's Café where I host a bi-monthly open mic, fellow writers and familiar café patrons asked me what happened. A few offered one of those telltale winks; others asked me if I'd been out dancing.

"Yeah," I told them. I've been doin' the Nanowrimo!"

"I don't know that one," a few people responded. Others shook their heads. One friend winked, thinking it was a euphemism for...well, you know (wink-wink).

What ensued was my explanation (too long-winded to include here) of how I was "in the zone" for about seven hours, sitting in my dilapidated office chair, with what was obviously poor posture (i.e., alternately sitting with my foot under my derriere, half-lotus, full-lotus, slung over the handrails—who knows what other body-defying contortions I attained!).

"Better put some ice on that," one of my well-meaning friends suggested. "Alternate that ice with heat," a nearby patron countered.

I don't know about you, but when I'm "in the zone", I forget about my body unless it screams for food, air, coffee, clove cigarettes—or whatever else it thinks it needs. I love being in the zone. The words just flow out of my mind, through my fingers, and onto the screen. Being in the zone even for a day makes up for all those other days when each and every word laughs at me because it can't believe I actually have the audacity to even type it—much less keep it in the file. Being in the zone for even an hour makes up for all those hours I lie awake in bed playing around with plots and characters and setting and dialogue, etc. Being in the zone for even a few minutes is like a mega dose of B-12 vitamins, as it can put me in such a good mood that I forget all those other issues (e.g., paying bills, doing laundry, finding a new job, etc.).

Of course I'll "finish" the NaNoWriMo. As to whether my novel-in-process is good, let's just say it has potential. Ask me if it has a plot, and I'll tell you that I expect to uncover it by the time this draft is done. Hopefully.

As to my poor writing posture, I'm trying really, really hard to sit up straight, shoulders back, chest open, and head dangling from that invisible string, but I feel my feet and fingers twitching to do the Nanowrimo...(Thank goodness for body workers, acupuncturists, kung fu, bak fu pai, and yoga!)

If you'd like to explore the wacky world of writing without a plot you've absolutely got to get Chris Baty's guidebook: *No Plot? No Problem!* I guarantee you'll be inspired!

If you're not busy doin' the NaNoWriMo, then maybe you could provide support for someone who is. You can clean their house, bring them prepared meals, coffee, and lots of chocolate. You could also take their kids to school, pick them up, assist them with homework, read them a bedtime story, then put them to bed. NaNoWriMo-ers will really appreciate your efforts—and promise not to snarl at you when they receive your countless perky phone calls, messages, and emails letting them know how much more time and how many more words they have to get to that "finish" line.

Draft two? Hey Chris, if you're reading this, maybe we could have a NaNoWriMo boot camp throughout the year...

Home for the Holidays?
Write About it!

Looking for some inspiration? You don't need to look any further than the person sitting next to you at the dinner table. Ok, maybe across the table. Okay, maybe across the street. All right! They live out of town and you haven't seen them for years. Or maybe you just got off the phone with them, and they're coming to stay with you for a week or two or three. . .

Who are they?

Why they're your family: immediate, extended, blended, adopted, or created!

You've no doubt heard the oft-repeated adage: write about what you know. I believe that extends to write about **who** you know. Imagine the possibilities!

One of great things about have family—however you define them—is that they're a virtually bottomless well of excellent material from which to create fiction (or non-fiction, but that's another column). Another plus is that you have the physical, mental, and emotional commentary from other family members from which to draw. What do I mean by that? Just call up your sister or your brother or your mother and ask them a seemingly innocuous question such as, "How do you make mushroom gravy?", or, "why do you think uncle so-and-so disappeared for three hours when he said he was only going to the store for ice?", to know what I mean.

Remember those flip books to make silly creatures? I love them. You can do it with people and their beloved quirks, too. Here's how:

1. Fold a piece of paper into three columns. You can also use a WORD page, or EXCEL or the table function. 3x5 cards are also great if you like stiffer paper to shuffle. You could also cut these cards into fours.
2. In column one, write a list of family members, friends, etc. (note: be sure to leave space in between each item as you're going to be cutting them out.)
3. In column two, create a list of their attributes, quirks, etc.
4. In column three, create a list of things they've said, such as adages, cooking tips, or advice.
5. Cut them out by category (Oh go ahead—color coordinate them, too. Red for people, blue for attributes, orange for snippets of dialogue).
6. Shuffle and lay them face down.
7. Take one from the people pile, one from the characteristic's pile, and one from the dialogue pile, then lay them face up.

Write this material in a note book or word file under the heading of "character bios"—or whatever works for you.

8. Get out your "writers license" and add in other quirks from other characters. Ask yourself what motivates them, what they want, what they don't want, etc.
9. Now write a little drabble (100-word short story—exactly100 words, no more, no less...not counting the title), a flashshot (no more than 110 words), a piece of sudden or flash fiction (Word counts vary. Some say they're no more than 1,000, others, no more than 500. I like the 200-500-word variety.)
10. Do another one.
11. Go ahead! Do another one and another one and another one. Before you know it, you will have peopled an entire universe.

After the holidays—or even during—you can edit and revise while feasting on all those left-overs...You'll have a veritable cornucopia of short stories in process! So, next time your family gathers, having now read your short story or novel, and they're "up in arms" or "incredibly delighted" that they're in it, you can point to that little disclaimer that says: "This is a work of fiction. Any resemblance to real events or real people is pure coincidence" then shrug and smile. After all, writing fiction is often like a crazy quilt; we piece it together as we move along.

Oh—before I forget. . .I suggest you change their names—just in case!

Here's a mish-mash from one of my three-part column exercises (and yes, I'm playing it safe!):

Name	Attributes	Sayings
Uncle Lee	Gourmet chef specializing in French and Louisiana-style cusine	Spelled "Mississippi" M-i-crooked letter-crooked letter-i-crooked letter-crooked letter-i-hump-backed letter-hump-backed letter-i
Uncle Swampy	Had a gator farm	Laughed a lot
Auntie Karol	Has a thing for maps	"So what do you think about that?"
Timmers	Experimented with hydroponic gardening	"Your sense of humor will keep you sane!"

After I cut this up and shuffled it around, I had Auntie Karol experimenting with hydroponic gardening, altered states of consciousness and laughing all the time. Uncle Swampy had a thing for maps and mumbled "M-i-crooked letter-crooked letter-i-crooked letter-crooked letter-i-humped back letter-hump backed letter-I". Uncle Lee had an alligator farm and said, "Your sense of humor will keep you sane", and last, but not least, Timmers was a gourmet chef who asked everyone, "So what do you think about that?"

There's got to be at least four good stories there!

You Know You Want to Write Drabbles—Here's How!

First, a little history. . .

According to Tyree Campbell, Sam's Dot Publishing's Managing Editor, the idea for the drabble contest publication, *The Drabbler,* arose when someone sent him a drabble for consideration as flash fiction. At the time, he was unfamiliar with this form, and asked for an explanation. Once he learned about drabbles, Campbell realized that they were well-suited for a competition!

According to Campbell, "the idea of themes just fell into place. " He also thought that they would be fun to read and write. Furthermore, he "came to realize that a drabble is an excellent tool for teaching writing, because it compels the writer, in most cases, to make every word count--to teach the writer, in other words, to apply this to his or her other writing. So it's sort of like getting a writer to, metaphorically speaking, 'eat his vegetables'".

Campbell edited the first three *Drabblers*: Alien Candle Shop" (October 2004), "Alien Brothel" (February 2005), and "Eve and no Adam" (June 2005). The fourth, "Aliens and Forbidden Love" (September 2005), was edited by L.A. Story Houry.

Needless to say, when I first learned about drabbles, I was hooked, and probably barraged both Campbell and Houry with submissions. At that time, I was already on staff at Sam's Dot Publishing, and was thrilled when invited to be the contest judge and editor for Issue #5; the theme I chose was "The Three Moons", which is a reference to my Boortean universe. To the best of my knowledge, this was the first times my byline, The Boortean Ambassador to Haura (i.e., earth), appeared, and I have been honored to serve Haurans and the Galaxy at Large, in this capacity since then.

Since assuming the position of contest editor for *The Drabble*, I've chosen most of the themes, but have also taken suggestions from staff members and contributors. In case you're curious where we've been before, here is a list of the themes for Issues 6 through 19.

- Alien Employment Lines & Religious Practices, Combination Issue 6 & 7
- Alien Pet Care, Issue 8
- The Dark Side of the Moon, Issue 9
- Haunted Space Ports, Issue 10
- SETI received a broadcast, and this is what it said. . ., Issue 11

- Extra-Terrestrials on FaceSpace, Issue 12
- Alien Magic, Issue 13
- Special issue featuring Alien Sex secrets
- When Genetic Experiments Go Bad, Issue 14
- Living on an Alien World, Issue 15
- Alien Architecture, Issue 16
- When Food Fights Back, Issue 17
- 2013, Issue 18
- Climate Change, Issue 19

During the past six years, our primary cover and interior artist has been 7ARS, but we've also featured Cathy Buburuz, Scott Virtes, and Mitchell Davidson Bentley.

So, now that you're up-to-date on a bit of history, what, you may ask, is a drabble, and why would I want to write one? Trust me. . .once you find out, it will become a need rather than a want. . .

While our guidelines can be found at samsdotpublishing.com (under the drabble icon), here is a brief recap.

Basically, a drabble is a work of fiction, a short-short story much like sudden fiction (and all those other synonyms). The difference, however, is that they are exactly 100 words, no more, no less, while their titles may be 15 words or less (i.e., providing more words to tell the story – 115 total!) Yes, they are a challenge, and it's been my personal experience that a drabble may often take longer to write than the oxymoronic short story. They are also addictive, highly contagious, and are known to "go viral" (Sorry, there is no vaccine. . .but why would you want one?)

Drabbles can be fun, serious, contemplative, experimental, outrageous, ludicrous, oxymoronic, wry, maddening, bloody, and yes, they can cross genres whenever they wish—and often do. Horror, science fiction, speculative, cyber punk. . .you name it and they can be it.

One of the things I've observed from my own writing practice, is that a short story of 2,000+ words may be "better told" in a drabble. On the proverbial flip side, a drabble has the capacity to encapsulate a much longer work for safe-keeping—even a novel with sequels! Several contributors have told me that they use drabbles in this way, as do I.

If you have a stack of poems that are resisting completion, they may be trying to tell you that they're really drabbles! So, step back, give them (and yourself) some room to explore the infinite array of possibilities.

To illustrate, I've included one of my poems, "A Sighting", as a demonstration as to how it morphed into a drabble.

Here is the original mirror cinquain of 36 words with a 2-word title:

A Sighting

The sun
breaching the clouds
like a starship landing. . .
incandescent rays hovering
above

dark blue
waves. . .I pause to watch its descent. . .
there--just beyond the pier--
so delicate
the sound.

Here's the first draft of the drabble it may become. . .It's a bulky 121 words with a 3-word working title.

Alien Landing Bay

The lights along the Ocean Beach pier aren't for romantic walks by moonlight. Actually, they're beacon lights to guide alien ships to their underwater station.

How do I know this?

Because my boyfriend was abducted by one just the other night.

We were walking along the pier, the sun breaching the clouds like a starship landing, incandescent rays hovering above dark blue waves. We paused to watch the sunset, there—just beyond the pier.

And then I heard a sound, delicate, like the alighting of a seagull on silvery sand.

Then whoosh--and he was gone without a splash.

I called 911, but they didn't believe me, and so here I lean at pier's end, watching the sky for another sighting.

END

And here's the second draft (or maybe it's the fifth, as I often lose count of revisions even though I save most of them. . .) that comes in at 98 words with a new 8-word title.

My boyfriend was abducted by aliens the other night

How do I know?

Because I was with him.

We were walking along the Ocean Beach Pier just around sunset, where indigo, fuchsia, and gold striations still hovered above the horizon. We held hands, leaned into each other, kissed, as waves of fog swirled around us.

There was a delicate sound, like sea foam dissolving at shore's edge, and when the fog cleared, my boyfriend was no longer in my arms, wrenched away without so much as a sharp intake of breath.

My boyfriend was abducted by aliens the other night.

I should know, as I was there.

END

All I need now is two more words, but I'm not sure if I like the tone of the title, and want to have more of a plot. I'm also not sure if I should use the frame (i.e., ending with the title and a response to the question).

Here's the third (or seventh) draft. I will probably sit with for a while before "finishing" it.

What Really Happened at the Ocean Beach Pier That Night?

Seth and I were walking along the worn wooden pier, not-the-least bothered by screeching seagulls and an encroaching fog. We scanned the horizon, hoping to finally see the green flash at sunset.

We kissed, closing, then opening our eyes to a lightning-flash of emerald green, to odd red objects hovering.

Seth clambered up on the railing, reached out for one of the floating obelisks. . .

Then I swear the waves rose above the pier like the tentacles of a giant octopus, or the petals of a lily, to engulf him.

And no, I never heard a splash. . .

I hope the above illustration demonstrates how drabbles are like genetic mutations encoded with the will to survive AND proliferate! I look forward to reading yours, and don't forget that I'm open to thematic suggestions for upcoming contests!

If you've submitted over and over and over again, and haven't yet appeared in *The Drabbler,* there may be several reasons for this. Here are just a few in non-hierarchical order:

1. You're using one of those drabble generators;

2. All (or most) of your drabbles sound the same;

3. You aren't reading the guidelines;

4. You're not making note of the theme;

5. You're stretching the theme out so far that it has boomeranged back to where you started (i.e., the blank page);

6. You only send one per contest period and it didn't grab the Boortean Ambassador;

7. The Boortean Ambassador couldn't make sense of the drabble, and even though she is reasonably bright, didn't think that others would make sense of it, either;

8. The Boortean Ambassador already read a dozen very similar drabbles, and alas, yours wasn't the chosen one;

9. There were multiple errors and the story didn't make up for them (and yes, The Boortean Ambassador will occasionally conduct minor edits when the story is too good to pass up!);

10. The drabble has been published before;

11. The drabble has been submitted to a previous drabble contest, and while the treatment may fit the current theme, one of the above may still apply;

12. There is no story;

13. You thought you submitted it, but you just dreamt that you did;

14. You submitted it, but it was devoured by the dragon at universe's edge;

15. You sent it to The Boortean Embassy during a service provider change-over;

16. You don't read the samsdotpublishing.com bulletin board or FaceBook page where The Boortean Ambassador will post urgent messages such as deadline changes, updated email addies, and so forth;

17. You waited until the day of the deadline, and the Muse was in a bad mood;

18. You didn't fill in the "subject" line, and your drabble was summarily deleted; and

19. There is probably another reason The Boortean Ambassador hasn't thought of-yet!

And remember to visit samsdotpublishing.com regularly! Just click on the "Drabbler" icon to be whisked away to trans-galactic adventures via the contest guidelines, and the winners, as well as new contest themes, are posted in "At the Dot", our monthly newsletter.

Disclaimer: Neither Sam's Dot Publishing nor *The Drabbler* editor, or The Boortean Embassy and its various interests, sponsors, and/or subsidiaries, are responsible for genetic experiments that breach their containment fields. Please to contact the proper local authorities in the event that this should happen.

Using Numerology to Create Character Names

While the ancient system of numerology has been used for naming newborn babies, it can also be used to name and provide a profile for your gestating characters.

One of the hallmarks of a good writer is not only creating memorable characters, but creating names that suit their nature and behavior. While some characters reveal their names without too much prodding, other times, they may resist sharing their names until the writer gets to know them better. Then there are those characters who, for whatever reason, adamantly refuse to utter their names. . . Much like in the case of the fabled Rumplestilskin, the writer may need to use a bit of magic and divination or otherwise appeal to otherworldly forces.

Creating Names for an Ongoing Series

When writers are planning to pen a series featuring an ongoing protagonist, then they want to create a name that will resonate throughout the series and possess that proverbial household ring. Consider the popularity of prolific *New York Time's* Best-Selling author, Nora Roberts' speculative murder mystery series that takes place forty-plus years hence in an imagined future that still bears a strong resemblance to current times – but with an edge. With approximately twenty novels in this series, Roberts, writing as J.D. Robb, has created an addictive series with her protagonist Eve Dallas. The series includes titles such as *Creation in Death, Promises in Death*, and the recently released *Indulgence in Death* – all available from her website, and with commentary and "sneak peeks" at jdrobb.com.

A Brief Numerological Analysis of J.D. Robbs' Protagonist, Eve Dallas

While the success of this series is due to a variety of reasons, which include lots of crime-solving action, a circle of intriguing friends, not to forget, her conflict-ridden love-interest, consider for a moment, the numerological analysis of the name, Eve Dallas. While this is only a brief summary of what Paul Sadowski's free numerological site revealed, this writer/reader believes it encapsulates many facets of Dallas' personality, and provides some insight into why she acts -- or refrains from acting – in many instances.

The analysis provided the number nine, and its characteristics are "Humanitarian, giving nature, selflessness, obligations, creative expression" (Sadowski). The "expression" of these characteristics is further discussed, and includes both positive and negative aspects. "If you are able to achieve the potential of your natural expression in this life," for example, "you are capable of much human understanding and have a lot to give to others. Your personal ambitions are likely to be maintained in a very positive perspective, never losing sight of an interest in people, and a sympathetic, tolerant, broad-minded and compassionate point of view. You are quite idealistic, and disappointed at the lack of perfection in the world. You have a strong awareness of your own feeling as well as those of others. Friendships, affection, and love are extremely important" (Sadowski).

If "[u]ndeveloped or ignored," however, "the negative side. . .can be very selfish and self-centered. If you do not actively involve yourself with work that benefits others, you may tend to express just the opposite characteristics. It is your role to be very involved with other people and their needs, but it may be difficult for you achieve this role. Aloofness, lack of involvement, and a lack of sensitivity mark the low road of this expression" (Sadowski).

For those of you who have read this series, the above may sound quite familiar, as Lt. Dallas often battles the inner demons and quandaries above. Did Ms. Robb use numerology to arrive at this character name, or did Eve herself reveal it? Since I'm not acquainted with the author, I don't know. Regardless, it is intriguing how closely, in this reader's perspective, the above reveals part, but not all, of who Eve Dallas is as a person and what motivates her.

Exploring Numerology

There are hundreds, perhaps thousands, of free-access numerology sites with articles and name generators on the web. While some, as the saying goes, are better than others, and there are those with hidden fees and trial memberships which you may want to avoid. . .If you're stuck on a character's, or set of characters' names, then why not experiment with this excellent tool? This exercise may also assist with creating plot turns and twists, as well as other necessary story development essentials.

Additional Resources:
Keller, Joyce and Jack Keller. *The Complete Book of Numerology. New York:* St. Martins, 2001.
McClain, Micael. "Numerology." Astrology-numerology.com. Web.
Works Cited
Roberts, Nora. NoraRoberts.com. Web.
Sadowski, Paul. "Numbers." PaulSadowski.com. web.

Cherry-Chocolate Bloodsicles - How to Create a Title for Your Story

This piece was previously published online at suite101.com under "How to Create a Title for Your Story" on September 29, 2010.

Titles are one of the first things an editor or a reader will see. They are more than just place-holding labels.

Titles possess the power, both latent and potential, not only to draw a reader in, but to mesmerize them throughout the story and beyond its supposed end. A good story title becomes more than just a slogan or an adage; it has the capacity to be a spell, the mere utterance of which binds the story to its past, present, and future readers.

Titles for Drabbles and other Microfictions

As the editor of Sam's Dot Publishing's *The Drabble* contest publication, I see hundreds of microfiction titles per year. While a drabble must be exactly 100 words, no more, no less, its title may be up to 15 words! This not only provides a writer with additional space to tell their story, but it may also expand its scope exponentially.

Many writers have great fun with this process, and often come up with stand-alone titles (i.e., the title is the best part of the story), others continue to provide a simple two-to-three-word title. There is nothing wrong with a short title, as sometimes less IS more, but they can definitely add multi-dimensionality to a piece which possesses minimal words.

Which of these titles would you prefer to read?

- The Ordonian Love Knot
- Nadar Goes on an Extended Vacation, Thus Learning That There Are No Accidents
- What went wrong with the interspecies dating experiment?
- A Cherry-chocolate-covered bloodsicle
- What Really Happened at the Roswell Crash

While all but one of the above have already been published under their assigned titles, if I were to revise, I would change all of the titles but one: "Nadar Goes on an Extended Vacation, Thus Learning That There Are No Accidents".

Why? For one, because I didn't use all of the available words (i.e., 15); for two, because some of the above titles may be better included within the story to expand its scope; for three, they sound more like labels than a portal into an experience. While some people may disagree with me, and I may even disagree with myself later, at this writing, that is my honest assessment.

General Fiction Titles

While publications may accept a writer's title as part of the story, many editors will say something to the effect that they like the piece, but the title doesn't fit, suit their guidelines or even the piece's content. After all, one of the primary reasons for a title is to grab the reader and keep them reading - whether that reader is a single editor, a panel of editors, and/or the reading public. Choosing what to read in an anthology or other fiction publication is both a subjective and an objective process. Sometimes, a reader is in search of a favorite author, or they are curious about someone whom they haven't read yet. Other times, they are in a mood; it's like being hungry, looking in the fridge or in the cupboard for a food that screams, "Eat me!"

What if nothing screams out? The fridge and cupboard doors are closed, and the hungry person goes about their day unfulfilled, at least in that one area.

I'd like to see readers who love a story but not its title, write letters to the editor suggesting new titles. While it's obviously still the author's - and often the editor's - purview, it would be intriguing to see what readers would offer.

Genre Fiction Titles

Case-in-point, I recently submitted a novel-in-process to an online critique group. One of my readers said that its title, "Still Life with Pears", didn't sound like a horror novel. When I first began writing the novel, it was titled "The Missing Piece of Sky", which alludes to a puzzle in the story. I "stole" that title for a collection of my science and speculative fiction, as it seemed a better fit for that body of work. While "Still Life with Pears" does not have a haunted puzzle in it, the people who work the puzzle are themselves haunted. . .Will I revise the title? Perhaps. Another one hasn't been whispered into my ear - yet.

Some Closing Thoughts on Creating Titles

Whatever your current methodology for titling a work, it's important to consider the possibilities; keep a title file or folder. Whenever a title occurs to you, write it down and save it for future reference. Another way to get a handle on composing titles is to consider the story's plot, its conflict, or its resolution; these may also be verdant vines for plucking.

What Was Their Name again?
Memorable Characters Need Memorable Names

This piece was previously published online under the title "Memorable Characters Need Memorable Names", at suite101.com on October 21, 2010.

This piece discusses strategies for naming characters and includes anecdotal examples from the author as well as one other sci-fi writer.

Creating the right name for a character may be a challenging process. While some writers use - and trust - the first name that pops into their mind, others study name books and pay particular attention to name origins and their meanings. There are other ways to find character names, such as drawing from personal experience (i.e., friends past and present), plucking them from family trees like so much ripe fruit, or collaging them from a variety of real and imagined sources.

On Nameless Characters

Is not naming a character a cop-out, or is there something else going on? No doubt most avid readers will have encountered at least a handful of stories where the narrators' or characters' names aren't divulged. The reason, or reasons, for this may be that the narrator or character is clearly hallucinating, having a psychotic break, experiencing amnesia, or another condition outlined in the DSM series.

If a writer realizes they haven't named their character, however, and it really bothers them (or their writing critique group or an interested editor. . .), then it's time to take time out to come up with a name. If the piece is in first or second person, for example, and the writer is experiencing difficulties figuring out how to work the name into the narrative or dialogue, the character could refer to themselves in the third person if absolutely necessary. The title is another good spot to provide the character's name. The point is that they could be anyone.

Or maybe it's who they are, what they're being, thus doing, that provides a clue. Consider such shows as *Grey's Anatomy* where the staff often (and yes, without sensitivity in some cases, but that's the draw, isn't it?) label their patients and others in their lives with descriptions like "Coma Girl" or "Gall Bladder in 2" or "Old Guy Whose Kids Don't Visit Him". Nicknames and endearments may work for many readers and writers.

Using Anagrams

Sometimes, without quite consciously realizing it, our minds scramble letters in a name to form an anagram. This was a fun game to play as children, and may prove to be a subconscious writing tool. For example, when I was trying to come up with a character name for my alter ego in a novel, I took Terrie Leigh Relf and arrived at this: Tertu Fler. "Tertu" is actually Finnish for "Terrie" (or a name with a similar meaning, which is earth, ground, etc.), and "Fler was a cop-out, as it's just my last name backwards. So I changed it to Flare, in order for the character to appear as if they had a pen name or an earth name. (And no, this character really isn't me, but she started out as me. . .Just in case you're wondering, I am planning to change the character's name again. Right now, however, I don't have a clue, and so will take my own advise.)

Mnemonics and other Name Recognition Devices

In non-fictional social settings, some people always remember people's names, while others hear them over and over and over again, and no mnemonic device seems to assist them with the process of remembering. The same might hold true in fictional settings. Do you forget your characters' names? Do your characters forget each other's names? Do you remember your own? Or perhaps more importantly, do your characters know who YOU are?

Ironically, we may remember names from the lines of favorite childhood poems. There are two famous fictional names that I'll never forget. The first comes from an A.A. Milne poem, "James James Morrison's Mother Weatherby George Dupree, took great care of his mother, even though he was three", and a Shel Silverstein poem, "Sara Susan Cynthia Stout, would not take the garbage out". The sing-song rhyme pattern is one reason; another reason is the content of the poems and the images and emotions that arise from them.

In fiction, however, we may not want to have sing-song names--unless it's satire. Single names, however, work like a spell in the multi-billion-dollar industry of branding: Dracula!

Naming Science and Speculative Fiction Characters

This process can be even more challenging if you're creating names for aliens in Science and Speculative fiction, particularly if you're not quite sure as to whether or not you'll need to add in a pronunciation key!

A fellow fiction writer responded to my call for anecdotal examples with some exceptionally insightful comments. She said, "I wonder if there are as many naming processes as there are writers? Most often, I try to develop a name that fits the character (SciFi or human) by how it sounds (gruff, weak, complicated, confused, other) and by what it means in his/her life. For SciFi characters, their names may relate to their home planets (Seyfert from SeyTTT). Sometimes, a character's name is a play on a real life person's name or another fictional character's name. Hopefully, these names linger a few seconds longer than some others?"

To respond to this writer's question, the first time I met Seyfert from SeyTTT, I never forgot him! (Her? It?)

Over the years, I've met a variety of writers who claim to construct character profiles before they ever start writing the story wherein these characters will appear. This is an excellent way to work out more than just their names. These profiles usually include the same type of material as would appear in a "living" person's (or entity's) biography. Where were they born? (Or were they hatched?) Where do they live? (This dimension? The local morgue? Another solar system?) What color is their hair? (Or who needs hair when you have tentacles?) Their eyes? (How many? Where located? Type of vision?) Experiences that shaped their life? (Who have they haunted lately?) What do they do for fun? (Build robots? Scavenge for grubs?) Do they like their job? (Phlebotomist? Brain surgeon? Bagger at Rite Aid?)

Regardless of a character's name, even if it's an alien orb hovering over Ocean Beach at high tide, it is that character who needs to be memorable - regardless of the method through which its name arises.

Strap on That Tool Belt, Grab your Thesaurus, and Start Hammering!

This piece was previously published online at Suite101.com under the title "Tools for Writers: Working with a Thesaurus" on March 23, 2010.

Words are both tools and materials. When a writer possesses a variety of these, doesn't it follow that they are better prepared to write-and revise-their work?

It's not only about having a large vocabulary, however; it's about having the proverbial "right" words to develop the multiple layers of a story. If a story isn't working, there could be many reasons for this; in some cases, it may just be a matter of clarifying –and enhancing— the setting, plot, and characters, etc., with more specific, descriptive, or thought-provoking word choices.

While the following techniques may already be familiar, or obvious, to you, even experienced writers take time out from their writing to do this; it's not unheard of to become tangled up with other aspects of a story's unfolding and forget that simple solutions may often solve complex problems.

Word Choice Exercise

1. Choose a short manuscript to work with, then print it out. This exercise can also be accomplished online in WORD with the pull-down menus (i.e., under "tools", use the "track changes" function, and under "insert", use the Insert comment" function). Other methods include using the underline function as well as changing the type font color to red—or any other color that will stand out.
2. Circle, or otherwise mark up word choices and/or repetitions that don't further the story's development. Are there repeated words that act as "placeholders" for information that needs to be added later? Are there favored words that tend to appear—and reappear--on a regular basis? Are there verbs that could be "action-enhanced"?
3. Take a sheet of paper, write all the words that have been circled, then look up alternates in a thesaurus. Be sure to look up and write down the dictionary definitions of each, so that the nuances of these words are clear. Dictionary.com is an excellent reference as it has a thesaurus section as well as etymological references.
4. Experiment with a variety of these words until the "right" one slides into place. (Note of Caution: This process has been known to alter the entire terrain of a story!) And yes, this is a very subjective process, so be prepared to put the same words back in during your next writing session!

In addition to experimenting with word choice substitutions, journal about these words and their meanings. Maintain a story idea journal, as sometimes, all it takes is an intriguing word or phrase to generate a story.

Another effective use of this exercise is when the word count needs to be decreased for submission, as most publications have word count guidelines.

Word Choice Exercise Example with Revision Notes

For an example, here are the first three original paragraphs from a story in process, "It Was Raining on the Night in Question".

When the unseasonable storm hit San Diego, it wasn't a surprise that there was a twelve-car-pile-up on the east ramp. It was also no surprise that there were more than a few bodies intermingled with the wreckage. What was surprising, at least to the officers-in-charge, was the solitary survivor in the center of the detritus.

Along with the usual ambulances, police cars, fire trucks, and other assorted vehicles, were several cars that drove past the carnage, leaning out their windows for a glimpse.

Perhaps they all saw what the solitary survivor wanted them to see; after all, it was raining on the night in question. Visibility being what it was, how could they be sure? Perhaps the overworked and underpaid emergency staff did turn their eyes away so they wouldn't have to lie on their reports.

Revision Notes:

Paragraph 1: The east ramp to where in San Diego? Needs more specific location. What about the parallel construction with the key word/concept, "surprise"? Does this create an effective tone or is it too glib?

Paragraph 2: Does this paragraph need more detail to show what happened, or would this be better illustrated later? A glimpse of what? How much of the carnage should be shown? Should the phrase, "assorted vehicles", be removed? Does it enhance the paragraph or detract from it?

Paragraph 3: Do the adjectives, "overworked and underpaid", appropriately describe the emergency staff's state-of-mind in this context? Could there be a more effective way to demonstrate that they had a difficult time believing what they saw? What repercussions might follow if they told the truth?

Closing Thoughts

While there are many components to a well-told—or well-written—story, effective word choice is a vital element; a well-placed word or phrase can alter, enhance, or otherwise affect its telling. A misplaced word or phrase, however, may create confusion. If that is the author's intention until the proverbial "all" is revealed, then that is one of the hallmarks of good writing.

How to Let a Story Find its Own Point-of-View

This piece was previously published online at suite101.com on March 15, 2010.

Point-of-View makes all the difference in how a story unfolds. It is a videocam that zooms in-and-out of focus-and yes, it uncovers all those fuzzy areas in between.

Whether a story is in first person, with a narrative "I", in second person, addressing a real or imagined "you", or third person, with its variations in omniscience, viewpoint definitely determines a reader's experience.

First Person Narration

First person is one of the hallmarks of the confessional story. It can be an effective way to account for ongoing action from a single viewpoint. The narrator, however, may not know what is going on in the minds and lives of the other characters—if there are any—and so this viewpoint may prove to be too limited. Questions as to reliability may also arise. . .

Second Person Narration

Second person often receives a lot of flack. Why? In general, creative writing instructors, editors, and writers argue that the narrator might not be reliable. Sometimes, this may be an advantage, however, as it keeps the reader guessing. Tales of mystery and madness often utilize this device with dynamic results.

Third Person Narration

Third person is often favored, due, in part, to its objective potential. Variations include an omniscient or partially omniscient voice. Descriptive passages which provide context, setting, and other essential information, are often more manageable. It may be an excellent choice when a writer needs to "get into" as many characters' minds as possible.

Consider the possibility that each story has its own inherent point-of-view, and that it's just a matter of determining what that is. If a story isn't working in third person, try second. If that doesn't work, try first. If that doesn't work, try all three—and enter the realm of what is often labeled "experimental fiction". Be prepared for the story to change dramatically into something totally unexpected!

Try This Exercise

Choose a story—or a passage—in third-person. Revise in first person, then in second. Are the characters resisting the change, or do they ease into their respective roles? Is the plot enhanced, or does it "all fall apart"? Does the story's conflict sharpen? Fade into the scenery? What about the characters' motivations? Make a list of questions, comments, and other analytical notes—and be sure to label (and save) all these drafts to assist with the revision process.

A Revision Example

This Third-Person Omniscient passage is from the beginning paragraphs of a story-in-process, "Four-Square and Dodge-Ball".

Emma hung her head as she walked off the four-square area to slump against the wall. She felt like she was going to cry, but didn't want anyone to see her. She went to get a drink of water, wiped her mouth with the back of a sleeve. "I wish I were invisible!" she thought to herself. All the names they called her: whale, fatso, tubby, blubber ball, and piggy were true. She hated being fat. She wished she were pretty like the other girls, well, not all of them, because she really did like her black hair and obsidian eyes, but she hated being fat and freckled and—

First-Person. . .

I walked away from the four-square game and hid in the girls' bathroom. I didn't want the other kids to see me cry. . .Why did they have to call me whale and fatso, tubby and blubber-ball? They're right. I am fat and uncoordinated, always closing my eyes when the ball hurls toward me—or dropping it when I finally do catch it. I hate it when the other kids make fun of my freckles—"

Second-Person with a twist. . .

"Why didn't you catch that ball? It was right in front of you--all you had to do was grab it. I'll tell you why no one likes you. . .It's 'cause you have squinty black eyes and all those freckles. Why don't you go play connect-the-dots with yourself? Oh wait—I bet you can't even reach your own freckles 'cause of all that lard in the way. Why don't you just disappear? I wish you were—I wish I--were invisible."

After this revision "experiment", it was clear the point-of-view should remain in third person. Why? Because there are additional characters who will intercede on Emma's behalf, and integrating them into the overall story would prove problematic. This wasn't a given prior to this exercise, however, which indicates in part, that the story made its point-of-view clear from the initial drafts. It's essential for a writer to trust their process, but to also maintain an open mind so that the story can be what it wants—and needs—to be.

TMI? Seriously?!
On Writing the Confessional Story

This article was previously published online under the title "On Writing the Confessional Story" at suite101.com on May 20, 2010.

All you have to do is visit a bookstore, library, or online bookseller to see that the confessional story is a multi-faceted popular genre.

There are a variety of subcategories within this genre. These include stories that are primarily autobiographical, sometimes referred to as memoir, as well as stories that are based on, or inspired by, personal and observed experience. There are also stories, essays, and articles which focus on a turning point, or major event, in a person's life, the purpose of which is to inspire, or otherwise inform and entertain, readers who may share, or be curious about, those experiences.

Why Confessional Stories are Popular

Part of the draw of the confessional story is curiosity, isn't it? A reader is given an opportunity to look inside the mind and life of someone other than themselves. Whether it's a public personage who is "bearing all" about their life in Hollywood, Washington, or a Federal Penitentiary, or the proverbial "average person" who is offering to share their experience traveling around the world in a sailboat, or advocating for their troubled teen, it's an invitation to peer into their minds.

Confessional stories are also popular because readers may want, need, and/or otherwise hope that they are true. While the reasons for this will definitely vary from person-to-person, gaining insight and information to apply to ones own life may be at the top of the list for many readers.

Elements of Confessional Stories

A story may often be what is termed "creative non-fiction", however, which means that it is based on, or inspired by, real events in the writer's life. This type of story may be embellished, or otherwise follow, many of the conventions of fiction in order to enhance the reading experience. To distinguish between fiction and non-fiction, however, fictional books usually have the standard disclaimer that any relationship to real or imagined persons or events is purely coincidental.

Even though a work may be labeled as fiction, consider the possibility that some authors may choose not to reveal whether or not their so-called works of fiction are true, or based on their own life experiences. There's an old saying that a writer's first novel is usually autobiographical, but if you were to conduct extensive research, you may discover that this isn't always the case. While it may be normal for a dedicated reader to want to know more about a writer's life or what inspired them to write that particular book, the author may never divulge this. Why? For one, they may consider it to be TMI, or too much information. For another, they may not want to share this part of their process. Still another may be due in part to the limitations placed on memoir and autobiography to be accurate and true, and confabulation, even in the healthiest of minds, may occur; in other words, the lines between fiction and lived experience may blue or be forgotten.

There's also the possibility that they signed non-disclosure agreements. . .

When a story is based on real events, writers will generally engage in extensive research in order to be as accurate as possible. It may read like a work of fiction, or faction, for story-telling appeal, however. Even if the author experienced these events first-hand, the details and the players may still be embellished. If it is a version, or interpretation, theory, or other speculation about the truth, writer's ethics demand that this is duly noted in the subtitle, in the author's notes, the preface, the introduction, or in footnotes, etc.

Writers Ethics and Authorial Integrity

Given the controversial "true confessions" of authors such as Robert Frey, who appeared on Oprah's show to discuss his supposed true story, *A Million Little Pieces,* which was eventually determined to be a fabrication, the confessional story has received a considerable amount of negative press.

When marketing your short story or novel, if it's based on real experience, and you want your reading public to know that, be sure to come clean on which elements are embellished or totally fabricated. If you'd like that to remain a mystery, or are concerned about the ramifications of someone coming forward to say "that's not what happened", then don't claim that it's all true. An interpretation of events may be an acceptable explanation. . .When in doubt, refer to ethics guidelines, such as those outlined in The Society of Professional Journalists Code of Ethics.

One of many questions to reflect upon would be why do you want your readers to believe the book is "true" or that you personally experienced the events as they unfolded? What do you hope to gain? Having your readers believing it's true based on your ability to engage them in your skillfully wrought tale may be more preferable in the long run.

The Horror Realm

The Horror, the horror, the horror!

—Kurtz, from Joseph Conrad's *The Heart of Darkness*

and

Kurtz, in *Amazon Women in the Avocado Jungle of Death, a cult classic*

Scrawled in Blood

Dark and light are two sides of the same coin. We cannot have one without the other because they co-exist in a symbiotic and reciprocal relationship; their absence and/or presence is a scale seeking balance.

in the bedroom	angels
come winter	her wombs will spew forth gods

It is that tension, that conflict, that world-between-worlds that is so fascinating— the way shadows make mischief with our perceptions, seduce our bodies, minds, and spirits into believing things are not as they seem.

Cocooned
inside blankets,
she sleeps with the lights on;
come morning, her mother finds her
transformed.

We can "flip" the usual paradigm, too, where we open our eyes and there is darkness, close them, and there is light. But this internal world is not blank. So much is reflected there.

spring cleaning—
whatever became
of father's eyes?

The unknown is fascinating. We crave experiences—if only imaginary—of clearing paths through kelp and seagrass-infested waters, of saving those who can't swim from drowning in their own fears.

Swimming off the pier
she finds her twin sister
who died before birth

What about relationships gone awry? The metamorphosis that occurs when commitments are made, contracts signed, a couple's fate supposedly sealed?

scrawled in blood on the marriage bed –
not even death will part us

What about the dynamic process of chaos to order, order to chaos? Being out of control? Not knowing what comes next, being afraid of what comes next—and yet we invite this uncertainty into our lives…

so many pushpins on
the cork board. . .
nesting grounds

And so we peer into the darkness so that we may brave Nietzsche's abyss, Jung's Shadow, and Shelley's monster, and so peel away the layers to the essence of who we are.

in the mirror
many faces
which my own?

Some see death as a closed door—even a door slammed in their faces. But for others, death is a revolving door, a gateway to another realm, another dimension—or a parallel universe, perhaps. . .

waiting
at the Rim of Shadows
body exchange

Perhaps monsters are genetically encoded, some sequences active, others merely on pause, while still others wait for an external stimuli to activate them.

she was a normal child
once

Isn't it about possibilities? The fears that rise from the troubled mind, the psyche that doesn't know, doesn't honor, doesn't listen to the voices of social proprieties, that crosses the line separating mental health from mental illness? The voice that tells us to do the unthinkable—and so we do?

humming Mephisto's Waltz
she sharpens all the knives

What about the supernatural? Some admit that communicating with ghosts and spirits, exhibiting so-called extraordinary abilities is all part of the human condition.

In the garden, a full moon.
Night blooming jasmine
mingles with his cologne.
For a few moments, even she forgets
he's been dead for nearly a year. . .

Then there's the aliens...Our culture has them engaged in all sorts of benign and nefarious purposes—even altruistic ones. They've been known to abduct, inseminate, experiment with and otherwise enter our minds and homes. But maybe they're just lonely and need a date...

even Terrans
are smelling good
Boortian mating frenzy

Natural horrors abound as well, as recent and past events have shown us. Storms, hurricanes, tornados, tsumanis, volcanic eruptions, and asteroid showers...

stuck in an endless loop - emergency news

There is humor in the darkness as well. Irony. Satire. Irreverence. Just plain old-fashioned fun and delight! Monsters can be cute and cuddly—even greatly misunderstood. Perhaps we make monsters in order to understand how they work?

just in time for the holidays - Monster Dissection Kit

True Confessions from one of Horror's Many Lovers

How many lovers do you think Horror is currently juggling? What about in the past? Since Horror's been around for a long time and stolen more than a few hearts (literally and figuratively), I'd say its lovers number in the millions!

It goes without saying that not everyone who has been in bed with Horror will confess the deed. The proverbial, "I never kiss and tell", leaves many us to wonder if those who refuse to divulge their proclivities believe they have a reputation to uphold. Could they possibly be so naïve as to believe loving Horror would somehow taint them, that no other Genre would touch them "that way" after Horror has?

Jealousy, that many-tentacled monster (a wicked, wicked creature) has a tendency to show up when Horror is around. So, too, does Revenge (who, I might add, is a horrendous dance partner). If another Genre wants to mope about, why not smother them with love by inviting Horror to one of their gala parties? How long do you think the guests will be able to resist temptation? Sure, they may be a bit cautious at first, maybe even play hard to get, but I guarantee they'll be screaming for Horror before daylight seeps beneath the door.

You already know I've been Horror's lover for quite some time. I kiss and tell, too, and am apt to share all the gory little details until you beg for me to stop. I won't say it hasn't been a sacrifice at times, but "resistance", as the saying goes, "is futile". Horror is just so incredibly seductive, and I do so thrive on an-ti-ci-paaaaaaaaaaaaaaaaaa-tion.

When I'm alone at night, I just love to imagine all the naughty little things Horror has done for me. Where else might I shiver in the throes of a mind-altering chill, thrash about for just one more breath, then leap into the maelstrom where Chaos rearranges my atoms into a single perfect moment?

What do you think about when you're alone at night? What about your relationships with those Other Genres? Are they as lusciously honest as Horror? Do they bend the rules? Shirk them altogether? Take you places you never even knew existed? What about gifts? Do those Other Genres anticipate your wants? How far do they dig to unearth your needs?

If you can't sleep at night, maybe it's because you climb into bed with banal novels. If you're plagued with nightmares (or daymares), what you need is to be thoroughly ravaged by Horror!

It's just a thought…

If you're a curious person who loves to solve puzzles. Horror offers these as well. Perhaps you're even frustrated because after the credits scroll, the book ends, or the poem resonates off the page, you're beset with unanswered questions. Some of these questions may be as visceral as, well, an alien female laying her eggs in an eviscerated mate, while others may toy with the proverbial "what ifs" that gnaw at our psyche until we risk implosion—much like a star going nova.

Questions are a sign of intelligence, and Horror possesses

intellectual as well as emotional intelligence. While I'm not claiming to be a genius in either category, I still wanted to share a few of the questions that have plagued me. While a few of these were "just" passing thoughts, much like asteroid showers in the night sky, others have haunted and possessed me, and I in turn continue to be obsessed with them. Perhaps this is why I'm an insomniac?

- What if John Lithgow showed up at my open mic with a poem he wrote based on his experiences filming *Twilight Zone: The Movie*?
- How many takes do you think it took to get that bathtub scene right in *Constantine* with Keanu Reeves?
- What if Robert Browning's "Porphyria's Lover" was based on a true story?
- What if the spirits that haunt the local drive-in only want to watch the movie and smell your buttered popcorn breath?
- What if the ghost that follows you around campus just wants to be your study buddy?
- What if those alien chicks in *Decoy* succeeded in impregnating more than just that one cop at the end?
- What if shows like *Surface* are a vehicle to prepare us for The Truth?
- What if you discover you run a Bed & Breakfast for the dead?
- What if your next door neighbor, a lovely, glamorous woman, is really one of the lizard people?
- What if you move into a gated community, only to discover that your neighbors are all daywalkers in a pilot 12-step program for vampires trying to switch from fresh to bagged blood?
- What if it's not cats trying to steal your breath at night, but the dead?

Horror is a curious lover, and adores you even more when you ask questions! How else do you think it gains entrance to your psyche? How else do you think Horror is able to perpetuate its existence, and so your inextricable bond? It is this insatiable quest for existential knowledge that has enabled Horror to prolong your affair—that, and the fact it has the soul of an artist after feasting on your mind and body, carves your bones into intricate beads to wear as memento mori.

Why does Horror do all this?

To prove its love for you. I know you want to confess! Tell us all the gory details of your torrid affair with Horror!

Nature Gone Wild – Morphing Animals into Monsters

When my son was little, one of his auntie's gave him a mini-flip-flap-book, *Por-gua-can* by Sara Ball. No doubt you've seen these around. Children aren't the only ones fascinated by this early lesson in morphology. I spent quite a bit of time alone with this book, imagining how I would feel if I came across one of these creatures.

The pictures are divided into three flaps, so what began as a porcupine, with a few flicks of the hand and wrist, becomes a Platcuna, which is part platypus, part porcupine, and part iguana.

While the Platcuna may not be that terrorizing of a creature (unless, of course, it gets angry and whacks you with its bill, then bombards you with its quills), just imagine other combin-ations! Take the Landtofrog, which is a combination of land turtle, octopus and frog. It will hop toward you, its beak snapping, then… the slither-grope of tentacles, the gnawing suction, the death-enhancing squeeze as it draws you into its maw.

Why not take this one step further? Create your own version of a flip-flap book with frightening results.

If you're a "good" artist/illustrator, you could draw animals in their "natural form". If not, or if you just want to get going with this process, look for old *Zoo News, National Geographic* , or any other magazines that have pictures of animals. Cut them into thirds, and then toss them into a hat or a bag. You could also leave them intact, and then as you draw them from the bag, choose which parts you want.

Then, using 3X5 note cards, or any other form of paper, write down animal characteristics. Put these into the bag, too.

Now pull out three or more pictures and three or more characteristics. Play around with them. If something doesn't get your creative juices flowing, then dump them back into the bag and keep repeating this process as necessary.

Say you pull a rabbit out of your hat. While they are cute and fuzzy, imagine the opposite. What if this cute little fuzzy bunny lets you pet it then eats your face off? Why not add bat wings? A blood-hungry flying rabbit that eats faces and lurks in the rafters of your garage? What if it prefers mud to sweet-scented grass fields and tree burrows? Add in the hippo. So now you have a huge, fuzzy, blood-hungry-flying creature that stomps you into a pulp.

Of course, you're gobbled up after that.

Not frightening enough?

How about a pet goldfish that swims about in its aquarium without a care or concern in the world. The goldfish is treated lovingly with choice flakes, a castle to swim in-and-out of, beautiful coral and stunning rocks. Then, at night, it leaps out of its aquarium, morphs into a human-sized creature with bizarre appendages that crawls into your bed and spawns. Oh how it spawns…

You awaken in the morning, numb from its anesthetizing poison, food for its larvae.

Ew—gross! But still not scary enough?

Horror, sci-fi, and spec literature are filled with horrifying creatures. There's always room for variations on a theme. Ask yourself what you most feared as a child. That your mom's new cat would steal your breath? That your brother's beloved dog would tear chunks out of you? That your neighbor's horse would throw and then stomp you? That the python in the glass cage would somehow slither out and eat the baby you were taking care of?

Fear is a personal experience. Some people are terrified of spiders. Others, of cockroaches and army ants. Ask your friends and family what they most fear—then write up a tale that will leave them cowering in their beds begging you to erase the images from their minds…

Or better yet, asking for more!

Don't Forget to Breathe: Some thoughts on horror writing

Here's a little riddle for you:

Clue 1: What did T.M. Wright do with a computer?
Clue 2: What did Stephen King do with tourists and frogs?
Clue 3: What did Ray Bradbury do with children whirling 'round on a merry-go-round?
Clue 4: What did Michael Arnzen do with a very special tattoo gun?
Clue 5: What did Brian Knight do with mounds of snow?*

For the initiated, the answer to the above is easy to deduce; however, the act—or the art—of creating good horror tales may be less so.

The answer? Could it be the unexpected? The bizarre? Or perhaps, it's the ordinary made extra-ordinary. The merging of the simple with the complex. The juxtaposition of hope and fear. The impossible made possible. The unbelievable made believable. The proverbial "what ifs" that good writers will continue to explore.

Whatever the ingredients, I would venture to say that we know good horror when we read it because we FEEL it. How does this feeling manifest? In the tales listed above, my responses included the all-too-familiar fascination-repulsion dynamic. You know the feeling: at times you forget to breathe; bile rises in your throat; you can't put the book down (and yes, you carry it with you everywhere—especially to bed!); you forget to breathe; you dream the book; and so forth.

Horror doesn't only make us feel; it causes us to think, too. Deep thoughts. Thoughts we sometimes wish we wouldn't think, are afraid to think, but we think nonetheless. You could say that these thoughts stalk us through the dark fog of consciousness. The only way to dispel them is to read another horror tale—or write one!

Are you ready? Go ahead—take a breath, a deep breath. Don't bother to look the doors and windows, though, because horror can ease through walls and floor boards like a dentist's drill to a molar.

Without the anesthesia…

Here are a few ideas to extract a tale or two:

1. While good horror can invoke all of the senses without actually naming them, what if your protagonist is in a sensory-deprivation tank for years—or even decades?
2. Explore the senses: sight, sound, taste, touch, and consciousness. Bring in synaesthesia, or the hearing of a

sight, the tasting of a sound, etc. How might that add to a horrifying tale? What does a genetic formula taste like?

3. While many people keep "dream" journals, why not keep a "nightmare" journal. Our subconscious mind has a direct connection to the Dark Muse. I've used my own recurring nightmares as story seeds and plot lines.
4. What place(s) did you most fear as a child? As an adult? What about people? Animals? Objects? Events? Each of these categories could fill a volume or two. In elementary school, I was left behind on a field trip to the Star of India. The ship was calling to me. I remember being yelled at because I went into the "off-limits" areas. Recently, I learned it was haunted. I'm definitely going to revisit this experience—and the ship itself—soon.
5. Play the "what if" game with a writing partner. No holds barred. Record it.
6. One of my personal favorites I learned from watching Ray Bradbury's TV show. Look around your working space. What do you see? Each item—or person—is a story waiting to be told. For example, I know it's been done over and over again, but you haven't done it yet, right? The phone rings. You answer it. No one is there. What if this happens every time the phone rings? I know, I know. It's time to call the repair office. But what if the phone repair person orchestrated the malfunction?
7. Look through your "abandoned stories files". I know they've been calling to you. Go ahead. Read a few. Now revise them.
8. Study personality traits and quirks. What if your neighbor has a little girl who likes to tie up her Barbies—and Ken, too. What will that little girl be like once she hits puberty? I seriously doubt she'll outgrow this behavior, especially since she's been doing it since she was one-and-a-half.
9. Perhaps you're the scariest thing around—or so your friends and family tell you. Don't be offended; take notes. I'll admit that more than a few people get a bit nervous around me. Maybe I shouldn't tell them I dreamt about them...Then there was that guy who cancelled three dates. He said, "you're a writer, so work it out." I must say that he inspired a lovely evisceration poem. Haven't heard from him lately. Oh well...he's probably just busy at work.

The truth is that there's no one source of horror. It's a palpable presence all around us. There—can you feel it?

Just don't forget to breathe!

*In order of appearance: *The Last Vampire;* "Frog Season"; "Something Wicked This Way Comes"; *Grave Markings;* and from *Dragonfly.*

Mom! Dad! There's Something Under the Bed and I don't think it's a Dust Fluffy: How Monsters Take Shape

It's that time of year…

Maybe it's the pumpkins at the market or the black and orange M&Ms that inspire me. Or maybe it's all the fat witches smashed into people's front doors, the ghosts hanging from trees, and the lovely webs with delectable spiders.

It's not that we need a special time of year to inspire us, but there's something about setting the stage—the supplying of scenery and props—that nudges the subconscious to spew forth monsters.

Kids are totally in-touch with the monster realm. All it takes is the fine art of persuasion to convince them to allow you into their realm. Candy is an excellent motivator—so, too, are tricks like chattering teeth and foaming-at-the-mouth green gum.

After I stuffed her full of tricks and treats, I asked my seven-year-old daughter to create-a-monster. This is what she said: "The Attack of the Spaghetti Yarn Monster. It's shaped like spaghetti and then one day it comes alive and it starts tying everyone up and they can't get undone. And it's—oh yeah, it can trip some people if they want to knit. It ties them up when they knit."

I'd watch out for that one if I were you—especially if you have a few projects underway like me. (If I were to psychoanalyze the above, I think it would be safe to say that my daughter doesn't want me to knit around her…)

Monsters can lurk anywhere. Imagine dust fluffies from all over your house gathering together under your bed until they become a pulsing hairy mass that slithers up the side of the bed, inches closer, closer, closer until it covers your face, shoots writhing tentacles of hair, mushy peas, and stale macaroni into your nose, mouth…

The horror! The horror! The Hor-rorrrrrrrrrrrrrrrr!

Monsters can grow in your fridge, too. I recently cleaned mine and found a few scary ones that had camouflaged themselves as congealed syrup, salsa and onion skins. Trust me—if you encounter one of these shape-shifting creatures, surrender before they eat your face off!

Just in case you were wondering, your mother does love you. The real reason why she told you not to stand in front of an open fridge for very long is because you might get sucked into the Refrigerator Blob Monster's Maw!

One of my personal favorites is the Monster Inside the Drain. I know it's been done over and over again, but let me tell you about our Bathtub Drain Monster. It scratches at the bottom of the tub with long, sharp claws. Then, when you turn the hot water on, it scuttles away. You think you're safe until you pull the plug to watch the bath water get spiral-sucked down the drain. There's a lot of bumping about, the tub rocks and tilts as you scramble to safety. Then, a horrendous choking-gurgling sound as the Bathtub Drain Monster drinks up all the water, belching something fierce.

We've decided that's a compliment.

Eew—gross!

While these monsters may seem to be the common, household variety (and not particularly frightening), I hope they get your juices flowing.

Oh-my-goodness! Don't turn around. Don't turn around. Don't—

(Squishing-crunching-smacking sound)

Writing in the Dark

The winter solstice is fast approaching on Dec. 21, the shortest day of the year, when the sun will again begin to make its ascent toward longer days. While I usually bemoan the loss of daylight savings time, there is another part of me, that creative/intuitive part, that welcomes the dark.

Why?

It's not only because I love the horror genre and scanning the night skies for extraterrestrial cruisers; it's mainly because I write better when it's dark outside. I'm more focused, more reflective, more connected to my internal experience and all that signifies. I admit there are fewer distractions, or perhaps distractions of a different order: fires on the hearth, snuggly socks and all those novels I didn't read when hanging out at the café...Holiday celebrations. We "all" have our lists...

I can't tell you how many times I've heard people complain of the "blank—or black—screen" phenomenon. Some people refer to this as "being stuck", while others refer to it as writer's block. I've always thought of it as a *tabula rasa*, a blank slate, a field of possibilities. It's an invitation for words to arise.

If you allow yourself to sit with a blank screen long enough, words will appear—as if by magic (note: this is an "ordinary" magic, and there's no hocus-pocus or other spells needed. Usually.). Call it a scrying pond, if you like…We stare and stare at that computer screen, sometimes peering so close we can see our own reflection. (Perhaps the paper industry should invent a reflective paper for writers who prefer notebooks and journals to computers…)

But seriously, isn't winter a time of gathering into ourselves, of spending more time indoors rather than outside in the sun? Doesn't it make sense that it would also be a creative time? A time to reflect on that which was illuminated during "brighter" seasons?

I know it's been overdone to the point of cliché, but bear with me…Winter time is like the dark soil within which we can plant the seeds, or ideas, of future fiction, poetry, and articles. While many of these may not breach the top layer of soil, fully sprout or blossom for months, the process, or life cycle, has begun. Writing is a perennial, an evergreen tree or plant, isn't it?

Sometimes I feel that I'm a "night owl" during most of the year because there's that part of me that longs for winter's creative force. Isn't the dark energizing? Don't you feel that the moonlight quickens your creative petals to unfurl?

Consider, for a moment, that winter is a time of power in its own right. Barring certain circumstances, you won't be prevented from writing—even if the electricity is off! Here are a few ideas to get you started! Who knows, by first thaw, you may have the first draft of a novel completed…

1. Explore your personal experience of the seasons and how this manifests in your writing. For example, do you write better when the wind is blowing and the rain is tumbling down? What about after first snowfall? When the sun comes out, the snow melts, and walking down the sidewalk is like riding a rollercoaster?
2. If you normally write during the day, try getting up earlier, before it's light, to do so. You could also try writing on in the evening, after dark. Do this for at least a week. Do you notice any difference in your creative output? In the types of ideas that you pursue?
3. Conduct research on climes that differ from your own. Situate a character—or characters—in this environment. How is their life different now that they're catapulted into the Land of the Midnight Sun? What about months of total darkness? There are actually studies conducted on these factors; of particular note, are sleep studies and space travel.

4. You love to read, right? Why not visit your local library and stock up on novels, short story and poetry collections? Then there's also great books and zines about the writing process…
5. Take an online writing class. Join a face-to-face and/or online writing group or literary organization?

Before you know it—spring will be here! And as we "all" know, it is its own special time for writing…

Wanna See Something Really Scary?

Imagine John Lithgow writing a series of poems about his multiple character roles in *Twilight Zone, the Movie.* If that doesn't scare you, then dust off your old copy of *The Norton Anthology of English Literature.* Begin with William Blake's "The Marriage of Heaven and Hell", then read excerpts from Percy Bysshe Shelley's "Prometheus Unbound". Follow this with one of my personal favorites, Robert Browning's "Porphyria's Lover". If it's dark outside, and you're feeling a wee bit frightened, I suggest you take the flashlight under the bed to read another one of my personal favorites, Christina Rossetti's "Goblin Market".

Now it's time to get a good night's sleep. In the morning, pull out that less dusty collection by American poet, Edgar Allan Poe. I suggest reading him by daylight, preferably with someone else in the house to protect you. Unless, of course, you're very, very brave. Better yet, have someone else sitting close by. Horror loves company. Have them read to you (the better to hear you scream…) No doubt your terror will know new heights as your heart goes thu-thump, thu-thump as if it's been removed from your body and buried beneath your bedroom floor.

Still with me?

Bring in graveyards, mausoleums, dark and stormy nights, vampires, zombies, ghouls and ghosts. Add a bit of gore, an awful stench, the sound of something scuttling.

Doesn't faze you a bit, does it?

Then what about being buried alive or tortured? Betrayed? Something's scratching at the window. The phone is dead. The lights go out.

Admit it. You're scared! You're fascinated with this fear, too. Compelled. Are you sick and twisted? A member of a perverted group of social outcasts?

No, you're in excellent company. You're a horror poet.

But why the fascination? Is it catharsis? Are horror poets writing out their demons? Purging themselves of their shadow sides? Or are they spiritual healers, medicine people, or exorcists who reach into your body to pull out evil spirits?

Brian Knight, horror writer (check out his newly released short story collection, *Dragonfly,* which has been nominated for a Bram Stoker award!), had this to say about horror poets (stay tuned for an in-depth interview with him in Feb. 2003):

> Horror poets have it much harder I think. Horror is one of the strongest base emotions, but we live in a world that has been desensitized to a great degree. I know - I watched my two-year-old daughter laugh her head off during the "Pea Soup" scene in The Exorcist. People just do not scare as easily as they used to. Imagine trying to make someone shiver with 20 well-chosen words. Easier said than done, my friend.

I'd like to leave you with these two poems by Knight to illustrate some of the many faces of horror.

Eater Of Children

The world is an ugly, ravenous monster,
It gobbles up our little children,
And shits out adults.
Our own flesh and blood,
Raised to feed the beast.

I look at him with a forced smile,
"My boy, you are growing up so fast."
But what I think is,
"Stand tall my son – put on a brave face and get in line.
It's your turn to die."

Paranoid – 5th Floor Blues

I sit on my 5th floor balcony taking names and notes,
Faces hidden behind sunglasses and smirks,
        shaded by baseball caps,

Government Monkeys talking into their shoulders,
Chain-smoking another pack of cigarettes –
        they are watching me.

Mom is with them now – she's come by again,
While I'm sleeping, showering, shitting,
The man next door has a copy of my room key,
For a blowjob he lets her in.

She wants to find my little red book,
I wish she would leave me alone,
She steals my brandy and cigarettes,
They want to know the things I know.

What are you afraid of? Write about it, then send it to me…I'll be watching you, so be sure to close those curtains…

Location! Location! Location!
Landscapes Made in Hell

Looking for a unique setting for your next poem, short story, or novel? Why not choose a hell realm? If you ascribe to the belief that hell is a state of mind, and that "we" create our own version thereof, then the possibilities for fictional settings are vast.

Even those who don't believe hell is an actual place, still have a literary conception of it thanks to such luminaries as Dante and Blake et al. Some contend that it is located in the molten core of the earth, while others argue that it is an alternate dimension. While the Judao-Christian hell's climate is often portrayed as lava-hot, the Nordic Hel is beyond freezing. It seems that there is no in-between where hell is concerned; it is inarguably intense no matter what the weather.

The Greeks' hell realm had Hades, who was both a ruling god and the abode of the dead itself. Complete with the river Styx, the river Lythe, and other bodies of water, this realm seemed to lie just beneath the soil. It seems that hell could literally rise up to find you wherever you were. How's that for minding your step?

In Buddhism, there are layers of "hell realms" inhabited by hungry ghosts and other beings. When people make their journey through the Bardo, there are a multiplicity of distractions to avoid facing an intense and blinding light.

While hell could appear like the alley down the street from you, it could also be found in a chemical plant, an in-vitro clinic, or your local school board meeting. Venus, Saturn, or Mercury would also be appropriate locales for hell, as would a dead-end job where your characters, much like Sisyphus, are destined to perform the same identical task over and over again throughout eternity. Hell could also be getting caught in a time loop, where your characters are forced to repeat their same mistakes until they finally learn their lesson. It has even been portrayed as a place overflowing with chocolate chip cookies—but no milk!

What if hell is nothing like this at all? Since the concept of hell co-exists with the concept of heaven, the proverbial two sides of the same coin, we can't have one without the other.

So where does one end, the other begin? It's all intertwined, isn't it?

Why not put a new hell on the map? You can locate it wherever your plot—or your characters—dictate. Be an explorer. Journey through time and space, climate and scenery, plants and creatures, then "just" start writing.

Be brave in the face of fear, and who knows where your next tale will take you. . .

How to Write a Horror Cinquain

This piece was previously published online at suite101.com on March 25, 2010.

The cinquain, just as with other poetic forms, lends itself well to horror and all it spawns.

Horror, like poetry, by its very nature, defies boundaries. It can cross genres as well, and it's not unusual to find cinquains which focus on science fiction, speculative fiction, and horror themes along with more traditional and/or contemplative themes such as those found in Japanese haiku, senryu, tanka, and their English correlatives.

Adelaide Crapsey, Inventor of the American Cinquain

Adelaide Crapsey (1878-1914) is the poet credited with inventing the American cinquain. According to her biographical entry at poetryfoundation.org,

"Crapsey's poetry deals largely with the subjects of death and dying, a predilection doubtlessly influenced by her knowledge of her own terminal illness." Her sole collection, *Verse,* is a must-read for anyone interested in this versatile poetic form.

The Basic Structure of a Cinquain

The word, "cinquain", is French for "a group of five." In the realm of poetry, this translates to a poem of five lines with specific line lengths: 2-4-6-8-2. In keeping with Crapsey's style, compressed language, enjambment, and other devices are prevalent, but many cinquains defy the usual sentence-level logic and don't always follow traditional punctuation rules. While perfect rhymes aren't encouraged, assonance and alliteration are. Metaphors and other figurative devices are also encouraged.

Another key component of the cinquain is the turn, or a shift, between the fourth and fifth lines that is akin to that found in sonnets, haiku, and other poetic forms. This shift may present a realization, a summation, or another way to step back from a poem to see it from another perspective. It could also be referred to as a poem turning back upon itself in order to further expand its meaning.

Cinquain Experiments

Just as Drs. Frankenstein and Moreau loved to experiment, so, too, do horror poets! Fortunately, many of these cinquain experiments have been a success. These include the reverse cinquain (2-8-6-4-2), the mirror cinquain (2 stanzas, 2-4-6-8-2 2-8-6-4-2 syllables), the crown cinquain (a sequence of 5 stanzas), and the cinquain garland (a sequence of six stanzas where one line from each of five stanzas creates the sixth)

Single Stanza Cinquain Examples

This basic cinquain was previously published in *Doorways: A Journal of Horror and the Paranormal's* Windows to the Soul Poetry Contest, which won first place.

Dali's Nightmare

The doors
open sideways
then horizontally;

at last, he grabs the knob. . .sprouts wings,
takes flight. (84)

Here is a reverse cinquain.

Remote View

Vocal
command. . . coordinates: accessing;
living nightmare revealed
panoramic
vision.

Here is a linked cinquain.

Winter Solstice 2008 and Other Cursed Tales
(with apologies to Shakespeare, Blake, Ginsberg, and Bernstein. . .)

Madness!
Utter madness!
What lunacy binds us
to that golden orb in the sky?!
A curse?
That blood
with a singular madness runs?
How with each stifled howl,
the cosmos is
disturbed?
So pierce
me through with a
jagged stake, fill my veins
with silver. . .or I will gnaw you
to shreds.

Here is an example of a Crown cinquain.

la Isla de los Muertos
(The Island of the Dead)

Isla
de los Muertos,
where the ebb and flow of
bloody tides beckon us each year. . .
where shards
of bone
reflect the last
glimmer of dying suns,
where the brilliant halo of each
full moon
quickens
our impulse to
transform, to return to
the paradise of our true forms,
and so
survive
yet another
millennium or two,
amid the ruins of our past,
so that
we may
discover our
place in this universe,
where just a flicker of life is
still seen.

Closing Remarks and Poetry Markets

While some poets prefer the adage—and practice--of content dictates form, exploring the cinquain with its line and syllable requirements doesn't have to be restrictive. Enjoy the process of experimenting with this versatile form, and add it to your repertoire. There are a variety of markets that specifically call for this style of poetry, such as *Amaze: The Cinquain Journal* and *AHA!*

Poetry's cinquain page; while not horror genre publications, they are excellent publications to read and develop a sense of the form. Other markets can be found at Samsdotpublishing.com, which publishes horror poetry, as well as Ralan.com, which is an excellent free market source for writers of all genres.

P.S. On May 26, 2011, two days following the uploading of this article, I received a note in my Suite101.com inbox: "horrible it sucks it is shit." I want to thank the person who took the time to send me this poetic reply, and would have appreciated it if they provided more details as to how I could have improved upon the article. As an editor, I can only imagine that I have rejected their work numerous times. Then again, perhaps they just didn't like the article.

Work Cited

Poetry Foundation. "Adelaide Crapsey Biography." poetryfoundation.org. Web. 24 March 2010.

The Postmodern Horror Film

(Or something I wrote in grad school and subsequently revised that I thought you might like to read. . .)

This piece was previously published online at suite101.com on August 30, 2010.

This is a discussion of Tania Modelski's essay, "The Terror of Pleasure: The Contemporary Horror Film and Postmodern Theory".

Tania Modelski's essay, "The Terror of Pleasure: The Contemporary Horror Film and Postmodern Theory" opens with a reference to Karl Marx that likens the capitalist to a werewolf. The hunger of this werewolf is such that it replaces living with dead labor, which is a reference to the replacement of humans with technology. This is an aspect of the fantasy of the American Dream: if you work hard enough, you will eventually be able to live a life of luxury, which is free from "burdensome toil" (155.)

Cinema, Bread and Circuses

According to Modelski, various critics have claimed that this freedom from toil which technology has granted us, "has resulted in the invasion of people's mental, moral and emotional lives, and thus has rendered them incapable of desiring change"(155). In a sense, technology, and its cinematic bi-products, is an opiate for the masses.

Modelski refers to Jacques Ellul, who discusses the development of "techniques of amusement", and states that, "it became indispensable to make urban suffering acceptable by furnishing amusements, a necessity which was to assure the rise, for example, of a monstrous motion picture industry" (155). The price of this amusement, however is a dulling of awareness, which results, according to Ellul, in "spiritual zombeism".

True pleasure is not offered to the masses; rather, a simulacrum of pleasure is. What then occurs is that mass culture is personified as "the monster". Mass culture, Modelski contends, has been ideologically transformed; where once we were aware of living an illusion, now we are sacrificing our awareness and consciousness *throu*gh conformity.

"Seduction without Consummation"

Mass culture is fixated on dramatic displays, she claims, referencing Barthes' "society of the spectacle" in*The Pleasure of the Text. This is the realm of un*known endings where pleasure is suspended. Barthes considers the desire to know the outcome of a text or a film, etc., as being a perverse pleasure because audiences will continue to place themselves in a position where pleasure is denied. It is seduction without consummation. Perhaps Modelski is using Barthes to explain that many movies, particularly horror films, are totally lacking in what is commonly referred to as pleasure. They are a sortie into pain, agony, mutilation, and so forth. The fact that these films are pleasurable to many audiences is perhaps an indication of a perverse nature.

What is the fascination with horror films? The dynamic of the attraction-repulsion syndrome? Modelski discusses "The Fate of Pleasure" by modernist critic Lionel Trilling, who speculates that "high art had dedicated itself to an attack on pleasure in part because pleasure was the province of mass art" (157). Furthermore, Modelski focuses on Trilling's argument that the "specious good" is the concern of the Modernist, and that the destruction of this specious good is "surely one of the chief literary enterprises of our age" (157). Postmodernism is seen as being in opposition to this good as well as to "bourgeois taste" (157). Postmodernism is adversarial, in that it "wages war" on such protected institutions as education, marriage, and other so-called family values.

Modernism versus Postmodernism

Modelski addresses Jean-Francois Lyotard's essay, "Answering the Question: What is Postmodernism?" and indicates that the difference between Modernism and Postmodernism is in their relationship to pleasure. She states: "For Lyotard, modernism's preoccupation with form meant that it was still capable of affording the reader or viewer 'matter for solace or pleasure,' [whereas the Postmodern is] that which denies itself the solace of good forms, the consensus of a taste which would make it possible to share collectively the nostalgia for the unattainable'" (158).

Lyotard attacks the notion of harmony (i.e., consensus and collectivity) as spurious because it represents a "cultural policy", the intention of which is to give the masses what he terms "well-made" and "comforting" works of art. (158) The horror film is far from comforting. It is, perhaps, a cathartic or surrogate experience—even a homeopathic one, where the audience is subjected/injected with the poisons of society in the hopes that the disease/dis-ease will be purged from their consciousness. They choose to have fear and terror, even madness, invoked in a "safe" environment, so that this fantasy becomes a reality they can leave behind once the film credits begin to roll.

According to Matei Calinescu, whom Modelski discusses, the audience experiences an illusion which is ideologically manipulated by a "promise of equally false and insipid pleasures" (158). Yet the masses are addicted to the notion of pleasure, and will go to incredible extremes to obtain what is nothing more than a semblance, or illusion of, pleasure. A facsimile, rather than an authentic experience.

Modelski discusses over ten films in some detail, and they are noteworthy due to their attack on what "bourgeois culture" deems sacred. They are also reminiscent of the uncensored fairy or cautionary tale. Here are four of the films which she addressed.

The Brood

Directed by David Cronenberg, staring Samantha Eggar, is a film in which 'Eggar eats her own afterbirth while midget clones beat grandparents and lovely young school teachers to death with mallets' (158). Trilling comments that 'Pleasure in the perjorative sense is sometimes personified as a female deity' (163). Modelski comments that the school teacher (as woman) represents pleasure; therefore, she is literally "beaten to death" because pleasure (in the form of woman) must be destroyed.

The Texas Chainsaw Massacre

This film has "actually been celebrated for [its] adversarial relation to contemporary culture and society" (159). Basically, it is about a "family of men" who have turned to cannibalism due to technological advances which have forced them out of the slaughterhouse business. They pursue (more specifically, the character, Leatherface) and murder a group of travelling teenagers. The last survivor, Sally (who is also blond and stereotypically pretty), is pursued by Leatherface. Does the "pretty blond" survive?

According to Robin Wood, this is "a critique of capitalism, since the film shows the horror both of people quite literally living off of other people, and of the institution of the family, since it implies that the monster is the family" (159).

Dawn of the Dead

George Romero's film depicts zombies as consumers in a shopping mall, engaged in what zombies do best, namely attacking and feeding upon the living. It depicts "the will-less soul-less masses as zombie-like beings possessed by the alienating imperative to consume" (159).

Videodrome

In this film by David Cronenberg, people are subjected to "massive doses of a video signal which renders its victims incapable of distinguishing hallucinations from reality. One of the effects of this signal is to cause a gaping, vagina-like wound to open in the middle of his [the main character's[stomach, so that the villains can program him by inserting a video casette into his body. . .'You must open yourself completely to us,' says one of the *Videodrome*'s villains, as he plunges the casette into the gaping wound" (159).

Mind control is herein depicted as rape, but the male body needs to be "feminized" in order to render him suitable for violation.

Modelski also comments on Brian de Palma's films and addresses the how sequels as a sign of feeding into mass consumerism, and yet it is another reference to the suspension of knowing, that delaying of pleasure's consummation. *Carrie, The Evil Dead, Halloweed, Friday the Thirteenth*, and *Rabid* are also referenced.

In closing, Modelski refers to Jameson's assertion "that art is no longer 'explosive and subversive'" "incorporate[s] images and stereotypes garnered from our pop cultural past" (164). She disagrees, and states that "Perhaps the contemporary artist continues to be subversive by being nonadversarial in the modernist sense, and has returned to our pop cultural past partly in order to explore the ste where pleasure was last observed before it was stoned by the gentry and the mob alike, and recreated as a monster" (164-5).

Work Cited:

- Modelski, Tania. "The Terror of Pleasure: The Contemporary Horror Film and Postmodern Theory." Studies in entertainment: critical approaches to mass culture. Wisconsin: U of Wisconsin, 1986. 155-166.

The Realm of Science and Speculative Fiction & Poetry

What if?
—unknown

Just imagine the places you'll go!
-Dr. Seuss

Science Fiction and Speculative Poetry?

All systems are go. . .

Why not plug in these coordinates to complete your mission of writing poetry.

Count down in T-minus 10-9-8. . .

So what is Science Fiction and Speculative poetry?

SF/S poetry explores the same themes as SF/S short stories, TV shows, and movies. Many authors write both poetry and prose. One of my SF/S-writing friends told me that much of the poetry out there is saga-like, in that it narrates a story. Bruce Boston, winner of a Pushcart Prize, a Rhysling Award, and the author of over twenty-eight collections of poetry, says, "it is a field with as wide a range as SF/speculative fiction, and you can toss in surrealism while you're at it."

You may remember my mentioning Tom Brinck's Scifaiku.com in the Q&A link section of last month's column. He is responsible for coining the term, "scifaiku", which is haiku based on science fiction themes. Oino Sakai, an early "scifaikujin", now publisher of *Starleaper* (currently being retrofitted for re-launch), where many scifaikujin found a place to dock, says this on how to write a scifaiku:

> In my view, you can't write a good scifaiku without at least understanding how to write a haiku. The better you know haiku, the better your scifaiku are. The easiest way perhaps to write a scifaiku is to write an ordinary haiku, then change the location to another planet. Or substitute an alien in place of an Earth animal or plant. Talk about a pretty yellow flower. Have it talk back. Write about harvesting rice. Have the rice colored lavender because the soil it was grown in is purple. Write about trying to explain Easter to an alien. Or just the Easter bunny, if you're squeamish. What's it like to celebrate Christmas in zero-gravity? Or near a Black Hole? Or phoning home on Mother's Day via a wormhole? Obviously, the more you know nature the better your haiku. It follows that the more you know about science and SF, the better your scifaiku.

Consider the following: ice crystals on Europa; the spiral and cone nebulae; green goo on asteroids; solar flares; waves and particles of light; space station politics; a launch count down; a space satellite lost in orbit; sex in a grav-free zone; microscopic sulfar-eating beings; shapeshifters; the 10,000 Martian words for sand; the socio-cultural constraints of inter-species dating; genetic mutations; cloning; being a host for a symbiote; the elemental chart;

Sheer poetry.

SF/S poets are real people in real time and space interacting with real and/or imagined experiences—and all those fuzzy realms between. The human condition? You bet? The alien condition? You got it! Scum in a petri dish? Sure. An intelligent rock? Why not?

Look what's in the bookstores (both on and off-line) what's on TV, in the movie theaters, on the web, in your local video/DVD store, on the person's shirt standing next to you in-line at the local grocery store or café.

"Who's-who" in SF/S poetry?

Since a poetry column by (my) definition needs to include actual poetry (rather than "just" a discussion of it), these poets form a constellation to light my night:

Star Whales

by David C. Kopaska-Merkel

The stars
are home to
Leviathan in spades;
red-hot beasts who stir their homes and breach (those are the flares)
in their exuberance.

They thrive while suns shine,
but when stars die the bones of giant swimmers surface,
in cold immensity, iron bones and chromium,
teeth of adamant.

But the whales lay eggs,
and these are highly prized,
for they are spheres like metal moons
whose surfaces reflect small nations without demur.

Eons, maybe, these will drift until they meet a star,
are swallowed up, and grow.
And if you find one send it sunward,
for the star whales bring good luck,
and love not now.

Alienspeak 101:
Coming to a Galaxy Near You Soon!

The star-slips land. Linguists, rhetoricians, and other parties interested in Transgalactic relations are there to greet them. The UTDs (AKA the "Universal Translation Devices") are switched on, ready to translate our respective languages. We engage in dialogue with our visitors, invite them for a double vanilla latte at Rebecca's recently opened café, followed by a jaunt, perhaps, to our famous zoo or a museum tour in Balboa Park.

It could happen, right? It may be happening as we speak, or sometime in the not-so-distant future. Meanwhile, a variety of writers—past and present—are busy creating—and recreating—language in order to inhabit their literary worlds. While this isn't the sole practice and province of science fiction writers, you're apt to find quite a treasure trove of linguistic delights and occasional oddities in their poetry and fiction.

Or perhaps they really are receiving broadcasts from other worlds…

Who better to assist in this linguistic quest than my alien friends! I also beamed out a call to a few of the alien-friendly lists I'm on, and quite a few poets/writers responded. Basically, I wanted to determine if they created neologisms, or otherwise tinkered with language, in order to create more believable worlds. In brief, I asked them to discuss issues related to the following:

1. the word and/or phrase;
2. its new or re-ascribed meaning;
3. a context (e.g., a passage, a stanza, etc.); and
4. the process (i.e., how you created the word linguistically, why you created it, etc.).

Many of the responders posed questions of their own as well as provided quite a bit of genre commentary. In the interest of brevity, I've highlighted a few of their comments.

David Kopaska-Merkel, publicist and editor of *Dreams & Nightmares* (http://home.earthlink.net/~dragontea/) stated that classic examples of this could be found with Anthony Burgess' *A Clockwork Orange* (1971). "In this book, as in many other examples of this practice, the purpose is to convey the impression that the story is set in another place or time. It is an effective method in the slang or other linguistic trappings if they are believable. It is easy to throw in words that sound like gibberish. In that book, "poke", was slang for sexual intercourse...This is just one example of the many slang words invented for that story. This word, like many of the others, made sense as a slang term having the meaning it had in the story, and added to credibility of the story itself. This book was set in the relatively near future and the slang was not difficult to understand."

Sue Burke, the author of one of my favorite short stories of all times, "Aliens Love Oranges" (http://abyssandapex.com/archives/aliensloveoranges.html, stated that she thinks "the best example of an alien language was in the *Star Trek TNG* episode 'Darmok' in Season 5, Episode 2. The Enterprise's 'universal translator' translates the words of some hostile aliens into English, but though they are all understandable, they make no sense. Eventually, Captain Picard learns their language is based on metaphors about their myths and histories, and when he finally learns their culture, he says, 'Shaka. When the walls fell,' and the aliens understand him and stop being hostile."

Teri Santitoro, co- editor with L.A. Story Houry of the award-winning *Scifaikuest* (http://www.samsdotpublishing.com), also mentioned Burgess' work, and says that "the first time I ever read a book with its own vocabulary, it was *A Clockwork Orange* by Anthony Burgess, who combined Russian with English, and came up with his own language for his novel. Then, I read *Dune* by Frank Herbert, who invented not only an entire world's ecology, but the vocabulary to go with it. I think that in both instances, the structure of the words and language not only placed the reader into the story itself, but into the customs and surroundings of that story. When an author invents words and languages, the reader gets drawn into something beyond the normal experience, which is something extremely helpful in building new worlds in SF."

While I have by no means exhausted the possibilities, I've concocted a few tidbits for poems, short stories and other excerpts which will all be part of *Coming to a Galaxy Near You Soon...The Boortean Embassy.*

Word: Sozar (So-zharr)

Definitions: 1. an expletive like "awesome"; 2. a swear word (depending upon tone); 3. said as a toast and/or to congratulate someone; and 4. something said in frustration.

Examples:
"Sozar! I can't seem to find the portal to return home to Boort."

"The Boortian Ambassador just hired you as her personal assistant? Sozar to you!"

Word: Poochi Bug

Definitions: A type of honey-making "insect" (for want of a better category) that flies but can also maneuver on—and in—the ground. Their tiered hives can range in height from a few feet to over twenty-feet. Circumferences range in size as well. It is believed that certain types of Poochi Bugs burrow deep into the ground as well. They are considered to be poisonous to most humanoid species. The Poochi Bug and its behavior is a rich source of metaphor in the Boortian language group.

Examples:
"I wouldn't go out tonight if I were you. . .The Poochi Bugs are too quiet."

"Please join me for an aperitif—it's made with the finest Poochi Bug honey."

"Those Terrans have much to learn about our style of transgalactic trade negotiating. They're larval at best." (This is reference to Poochi Bug larvae. Just prior to hatching, they wriggle out of the hive, thus leaving themselves susceptible to other predators such as the Mora Blossom. The Mora Blossom is a plant know for its exquisite fragrance; it exists in a symbiotic relationship with the Mora Spider, another deadly creature. Interesting to note, however, is that the Mora Spider's venom has psychotropic properties. There is also a belief that individuals with the appropriate genetic codes are capable of transdimensional travel once bitten.)

"You really need a vacation...You look like you've been building hives." (This is a reference to the Poochi Bug Hives which are constructed much like a village. It also references the underground activities of certain clandestine movements engaged in transgalactic political schemes.)

And we haven't even touched on body language! What if our visitors don't have bodies in the way we conceptualize them?

If all else fails, there's always telepathy. . .

If that doesn't work, then what?

Here are a few links to further your travels:

The Official Website for the Science Fiction Poetry Association:
http://www.sfpoetry.com/

Home base for the SciFaiku list:
http://www.scifaiku.com/

The home of *SpecFicWorld*—home base to a multiplicity of universes!
http://www.specficworld.com/

Strange Horizons—speculative poetry, fiction—and more!
http://www.strangehorizons.com/

Ralan's Webstravaganza—market lists, contests—and more!
http://ralan.com

Defining Speculative Poetry?
Let's Not. . .

What does the word, "speculative", mean?

Perhaps a better question, because poetry is both a process and a product, is: what does "to speculate" mean?

Well, it's an action verb. But what—or who—is acting? What type of action is it? When is it acting? How is it acting? Why is it acting? Upon whom is it acting?

You may have heard me say that the dictionary is not an "end point" when seeking the definitions—or meanings—of things. You're not going to find a definition on speculative poetry in the *Oxford* or the *American Heritage* Dictionaries. If you did consult a dictionary, then you'd discover that one of the definitions is: "to form opinions about something without having definite knowledge or evidence."

What does that tell us? Is it even accurate? How does it help us to define—or otherwise characterize, thus categorize, speculative poetry? Why attempt to categorize it in the first place? Because it's part of human nature to label, to define, to categorize, and thereby to "know" a thing?

But meanings shift. New things come into being. Poetry is composed of language, and language is organic...

Someone sent me an article where Ray Bradbury said that he considers himself a fantasy, rather than a science fiction, writer. I usually categorize him as both. Isn't the Heisen-bergian known/unknown dynamic at the heart of this? We only know what we know...

We can wax even more philosophical when considering the power of the mind...If we feel—or believe—that something is real, isn't it, if only to ourselves? Think of imagination, of those books and poems that have transferred you from your own world into another, that Sartrian exhange of author and reader. The meaning occurs when the two are connected...Or perhaps I should say, your meaning, your experience of the book or poem occurs then.

As you can see, I wasn't sure as to how to define "specula-tive poetry", so I put another call out to the SFPA. If you read May's Interview with the SFPA (see the archives if you missed it), the word, "speculative", was mentioned quite a bit and I failed to define it.

David Kopaska-Merkel, the publicist for *Dreams and Nightmares*, says: "Speculative poetry differs from main-stream poetry in focusing on subjects that lie outside our modern everyday experience. I do not think that the style or form of speculative poetry differs all that much, although it does tend to be less introspective and self-absorbed than some mainstream poetry." He also adds that "Steve Sneyd (who lives in Britain) is probably the world's expert on early speculative poetry."

As to the relationship between fantasy and SF, Kopaska-Merkel says that he includes "fantasy and SF poetry as subgroups of spec poetry. No one has ever been able to define either fantasy or SF to general satisfaction. Horror is some-thing different; its tropes are not like those of SF or fantasy; at least if one defines horrific poetry with fantasy tropes as dark fantasy rather than horror."

He offers the following poem as an example:

A Garden Adversus
by David Kopaska-Merkel

The tomatoes were whispering
At their end of the garden,
Huddling close so no one could read their lips,
And looking sharply over their shoulders.

One of the banana peppers sidled over to listen,
But was suckered viciously and forced to retreat.
All she heard before she was driven out of range
Was something about pasta.
Or it could have been "monster," she said.
The Romas are behind it,
The curvaceous Japanese eggplant hissed,
But the zucchini defended its compatriots staunchly:
It's those sots the Brandywines,
Or one of the archaic pleated varieties;
The Romans are far too civilized!

The zinnias could have been valuable allies,
On account of their clear vision,
But they remained aloof as usual.
Meanwhile, the plot thickened.
The largest of the bell peppers
Went over to the other side,
And the habaneros called for a preemptive strike.
Never mind that the Jerusalem artichokes were
Not yet in bloom, and the
Entire anti-tomato force was unprepared for war.

Suddenly, the tomatoes struck,
In a suicide attack that
Spattered the garden with gore.
The battle teetered in the balance, and
The lemon basil volunteered to sue for terms,
But the whole garden knew
He was inadequate to the task.

It was, in any case, too late:
The victory of the tomatoes was total.
Shouting that they needed "Leaf Room,"
The tomatoes volunteered in every bed,
And within a season the entire garden
Fell to the red menace.

(NOTE: This piece was recently published in the first issue of the *Birmingham Arts Review.)*

Sandra Lindow contends that "speculative poetry can bridge the gap between science fiction and fantasy." Her poem, "Mrs. Ezekial" (from *A Celebration of Bones)* illustrates this. She adds that it "was inspired by an article in *Science News."*

Mrs. Ezekial Writes Home

After we moved to Montana,
My husband's hand was upon the Rototiller
When he called me out of the house,
"Wilma, come see this, the garden is full of dry bones!"

He led me back and forth along fresh cut rows
Where I'd a mind broccoli and Burbanks would grow;
And I saw a great many bones, dirty white shafts and knobs
like broken porcelain bathroom fixtures
          jutting from the shallow soil.

Then he asked me, "Mother of My Children,
Can these bones live?" and I said onto him,
"Those who wore these bones, their time is over;
We live here now, let them rest."

But he gathered the bones,
First clearing the books from the shelves in the den
Then commandeering the dining room floor.
Six foot femurs, a four foot jaw; I stepped over them
          setting the table.

When he tried to connect them, he hadn't the knack;
So he said to the bones, "I'll show you who's boss.
The earth was laid like an egg in 8,000 B.C.
Your time was never, you fakers, you phonies."

And while he was prophesying to the bones,
There was a noise, a rattling sound;
And the bones came together, bone to bone.
Tendons and flesh appeared on them and skin covered them

But there was no breath.
Then I said to the father of my children,
"Remove that monster from my house before it breathes
And remembers what six-inch serrated fangs are for."
But he only replied, "Don't bother me, woman,
I'm on a roll!" and climbed onto my Duncan Phyfe table
Proclaiming, "Come from the four winds, oh breath,
And breathe into this one that was slain that he may live."*

And the beast** stood up, crashing through ceiling and attic,
A full forty feet of carnivorous flesh grinning toothily
Through a hole in the shingles, thigh-size forelimbs
With four hundred pounds each of tearing and crushing power.

The rest is history, you might say. The china cabinet,
  the whatnot,
The shadow box, the buffet, the dining set, all gone;
And my husband, best not get into that. In any case,
That's why I'm asking, Mother, for me and the kids to be moving back home.

*Ezekial 37:9
**Tyrannosaurus Rex—Order: Saurischia, Infraorder: Carnosauria, Suborder:Theropoda Family: Tyrannosauridae, Nickname:"the Schwarzenegger of Dinosaurs" <u>ScienceNews</u> 7/14/90

Drew Morse, an SFPA member who wasn't available for last month's interview, just completed his dissertation, *A New Discipline of Vision,* at the University of Oregon. The focus is on speculative poetry. Auspicious, isn't it? (Congratulations, Drew! Wish we could all be there to celebrate this phenomenal accomplishment with you...How do I get a copy of your dissertation?)

During our interview, Morse addressed the issue of narrative voice in speculative poetry, and whether it is authorial and/or fictional. He states that while speculative verse utilizes authorial narrative, that this is "equally true of 'mainstream' verse; the narratorial voice of a poem is almost always at very least a persona of the poet, not the actual poet speaking. And though there are certainly many speculative poems that construct fictional characters to be their speaking voice(s), again, the same is true of non-genre work."

In "Defining 'Speculative Poetry': The Benefits of *Not* Defining", Morse states:

"One of the most important things to realize about defining "speculative poetry" is that the genre is, and will probably always be, resistant to concrete, immovable definitions; the goals and parameters of the genre are in constant flux. This is one of the genre's greatest strengths—and a large part of what makes it so stimulating and illuminating to be an engaged reader of past, present and future speculative verse." He also discusses the work of Gene van Troyer and Robert Frazier's *Defining the Beyond*, where van Troyer is quoted as saying that "to finally arrive at the 'perfect' definition of a thing is to arrive at the death of the thing we are trying to describe.'" Morse cautions that "[t]his doesn't, of course, mean that it's not valuable to think critically about what SF/speculative poetry is and ought to be; it just means that any definition of the genre *must* be dynamic."

Morse addresses the relationship between science fiction and speculative poetry. He states: "The term 'speculative poetry' has arisen out of two desires within the science fiction poetry community: (1) to gain respectability by distancing the genre from SF's pulp heritage; and (2) to expand the boundaries of what kinds of subject matter and forms are appropriate for the genre." There is a "blurring of boundaries", he states, and adds that this blurring "is also the chief deficiency of the term 'speculative poetry'; what kinds of verse does it *exclude*?"

During the latter part of our correspondence, Morse indicates that speculative poetry has a place within "the Context of a Larger Movement". He expands this by saying:

"As your previous article makes clear, there is a fairly vibrant and active body of speculative poets—a speculative poetry "movement," as such (there are manifestoes, organizations, representative publications, etc., so I think SF/speculative poetry must be viewed as one of the more vital poetic movements of the last few decades—

though others, such as New Formalism/New Expansivism have certainly garnered more widespread attention.) One thing to avoid, though, is automatically saying that the movement itself defines the nature of 'speculative verse.'

In this regard, Ballentine's observation that 'speculative writing is not the sole province of those represented' in the genre's definitive magazines and anthologies brings to light two important points. First, there are a great many poets who write verse best characterized as 'speculative,' but who have not been recognized as such. There are also some writers whose work is considered representative of the genre who 'do not seek, or even accept, the designation' of 'speculative poet,' to borrow more of Ballentine's phrasing. Many poets, in other words, write speculative verse, regardless of whether they intend to—or even recognize they are doing so. (One of the joys of reading broadly—as a few of your previous inter-viewees suggested—is discovering just how many non-genre poets are writing wonderfully insightful and imaginative speculative verse; lately I've been entranced by the speculative poems written by Nobel chemist Roald Hoffmann; I've also been savoring some great speculative verses in the collections of Frederick Seidel, Diane Ackerman and Frederick Turner.)"

Thank you to everyone who contributed to this month's column. In closing, for some strange reason, I couldn't stop thinking about Aristotle while I was writing. I turned away from my computer to one of my book shelves and pulled down George A. Kennedy's *ARISTOTLE ON RHETORIC: A Theory of Civic Discourse.*

He states:

"In *Nichomachean Ethics...*Aristotle says that the soul possesses truth through five intellectual processes: epistēmē, or scientific knowledge; teknē, or art; phronēsis, or practical wisdom; sophia, or philosophical wisdom; and nous, or intuitive reason" (Newly translated with Introduction, Notes, and Appendixes. *Oxford: Oxford UP, 1991. 288.).*

Is this an origin for the adage, "writing from the soul"? Aren't these "five intellectual processes" part of what specu-lative poetry embodies? What of the "body of space"? I don't think we need a physicist or an astronomer to tell us that space defies categorizing.

On Speaking a Multiplicity of Languages
Or
Language is Something to Play With

If we spoke a different language, we would perceive a somewhat different world.
—Ludwig Wittgenstein

Language is as organic as that Venus Fly Trap on your front porch. It also has a voracious appetite...It is as malleable and impressionist as silly putty, the primordial goo that sticks to the roof of our mouth (and yes, to our fingers) like peanut butter. It is an architectural wonder like Balboa Park and the Coronado Bridge, allowing our minds to traverse from one park to another, one body of land to another. It is visual acuity in that it can zoom-in and out like a telephoto lens directed at a sunflower or a point in space. It is power, and can shape and reshape the universe into a multiplicity of dimensions.

It's also fun—like one of those floor-sized puzzles of the Eiffel Tower.

Some words don't seem to have their meaning altered much. They exist—and persist—generation after generation. Contrary to the epigram from Wittgenstein, we really do speak a different language, and our worlds are perceived differently as a result. One could have fun arguing that we live in a multidimensional universe as a result of language, and that as a result, we speak, listen, and know our world through a multiplicity of languages (And I'm not only referring to those languages associated with national origin with their respective dialects...).

Think: VENN diagrams! Each rhetorical community to which we belong has its own language and/or lingo. We create our world—our experience—through language; in turn, it facilitates our experience of this world, doesn't it? Families and other people who cohabitate or spend a considerable amount of time with each other come up with new words (and/or alter the meanings of words) in the same—or similar—ways that industries do when technological advances occur.

When an object is created, it needs a name; calling it a "thingamajig"—or other similar labels— will only work for so long...When an experience is had, comparing it to other experiences may work for a time, but what if it doesn't compare to anything you've experienced before? Doesn't it deserve, doesn't it call for, a new word to describe it? If we don't have a new word, and can't seem to agree upon one, we can point to that thing and/or experience for only so long. What if we can't duplicate the thing or the process or the experience? We don't want to forget it, right? We want to share it with others, right? Maybe we even way to patent it or make it or do it or share it.

It needs a name to perpetuate its existence as well as to identify its existence to others…

So, since neologisms, idiomatic language, and slang are thought-provoking categories for exploration (and also make for fun group projects), I asked my two summer school classes to assume they were linguists and contemporary socio-cultural anthropologists gathering and recording data. I asked them to discuss word categories, definitions, and examples.

Here are some highlights from their expedition:

Word: Lackies

Definition: Referring to people who just sit around talking about *Magic, The Gathering* card game, *Star Wars,* Pokemon cards, and play gameboy the entire day before and after class.

Example:

'Hey Chuy! Let's hang out. Just a minute…I have to ask this guy something.'

'Fine. So hang out with the lackies, you lackie.'

Word: Simon

Definition: Someone who tells you something about things or people with extreme exaggeration and later finds out it is a lie or is just plain crap.

Example:

'Dude, you gotta play this video game. It's freaking awesome. Anyone who's anyone plays this game.' Later, after buying the game and finding out I hate it and return it for a refund, my other friend says, 'Man, he bust a Simon on you.'

(J. P.)

These three slang terms hail from the Caribbean!

Word: Hey Ma

Definition: Hey Girl

Word: Skettel

Definition: Someone who has sex with a lot of people.

Word: Cockle

Definition: Another term for a female sleeping around.

These two hail from Hawaii:

Phrase: da kine

Definition: Used when communicating something implied, but too lazy to finish the sentence.

Example: 'I'm hungry…let's go to da kine.' This means the usual place these two eat together. Most people just think this phrase refers to marijuana.

Word: bannang

Definition: A person who looks Asian on the outside and acts white from inside.

(M. B., D.H., D.R., and D.W.)

Word: tight

Definition: likeable, cool, in fashion.

Example: 'Those new pair of shoes are tight!'

Word: turn-two

Definition: Get going. Let's move on.

Example: 'All right people…let's turn-two.' (NOTE: As you say this, make the "two" sign with your two fingers and flip your hand back-and-forth.)

(H.E., M.H., S.M., E.M., and C.F.)

Word: shema

Definition: to evoke empathy.

Word: sicky-gnar

Definition: good; overwhelming.

Word: M.I.L.F.

Definition: An acronym for 'mother I'd love to fuck'.

Word: gromm

Definition: child surfer

(C.W., A.H., M.M., and R.S.)

Here's one from Alabama:

Word: buggy

Definition: a shopping cart.

Here's a few from Minnesota:

Word: uff-da

Definition: Norweigian term used to express disgust or used in place of 'my goodness'.

Example: "Uff-da—it's hot outside!"

Word: Bucket

Definition: Another name for a woman's purse.

Example: 'Hey—look at my brand new bucket!'

Word: yaontoo (ya-on-too)

Definition: Do you want to or would you like to?

Example: 'I'm going to the mall. You can come if yaontoo.'

Word: Nambit (name-bit)

Definition: Norwegian term used to express surprise or shock.

Example: If something happens that you can't believe, you may say, 'Nambit—honestly.'

I don't believe these are from Minnesota…

Phrase: off the braken

Definition: cooler than cool

Phrase: That was bomady!

Definition: that blows your head, crying tears funny.

(B.E., A.A., I.A., and F.S.)

Word: shomgo

Definition: klutz; dumbass.

Example: 'I tripped over the curb and felt like such a shomgo.'

Word: snugs

Definition: cuddly dog

Phrase: Mickey Mouse

Definition: being resourceful.

Example: 'I couldn't find the tool so I Mickey-Moused it.'

Word: groovy

Definition: out-dated; out-of-style

Example: 'Man, look at her outfit—it's so groovy she should change!"'

(D.P., D.S., F.S., M.K., and J.P.)

Here are a two "lop-offs", or words that are broken up and stand for an entire word:

Word: inad

Definition: inadmitted

Word: depo

Definition: deported

Word: scooter

Definition: a motorcycle or a little car

Phrase: scooter trash

Definition: Harley Davidson rider

Word: skidlid

Definition: helmet

Word: spider

Definition: pubic hair

(S.M., K.N., C.L., and C.E.)

Word: Falcon

Definition: Calling dibs on hitting on a girl when with a group of guys.

Phrase: Junk in the Trunk

Definition: Voluptuous gluteus maximus

Word: Bangin'

Definition: A party that is the place to be…a tight party.

Phrase: Off-the-hook

Definition: Extremely cool.

(B.L., V.L., J.P., and I.A.)

Word: geterdone (get her done)

Definition: Go for it. Just do it. Motivational.

Example: 'If you want to become an actor, you can't lie around all day; just geterdone' (David Jaimes).

Phrase: butter face

Definition: referring to someone who portrays an 'ugly' face.

Example: 'Man, she has a beautiful body, but that butter face fucks her up' (David Jaimes).

Phrase: Jimmy Legs

Definition: Sporadic, or sudden outbursts while sleeping in legs (e.g., shaking leg).

Example: 'I couldn't sleep last night because she has the Jimmy Legs and she kicked me all night long.'

Word: teabaggin'

Definition: to suck someone's testicles

Example: 'She was teabaggin' me yesterday.'

(O.C., K.T., and D.J.)

Word: 143

Definition: 'I love you' (in text messaging)

Word: LOL

Definition: Lots of Laughs [NOTE: This is a separate, but similar, definition to "LOL", which in computer-speak translates as "laughing out loud".]

Example: 'The comedian, Steve Harvey, was funny. He was LOL.'

(I.B., J.F., A.A., and J.B.)

Word: winger

Definition: A long fall before the rope catches you.

Example: 'Hey Dude! I took a winger and thought that I was going to die.'

Word: P.F.T.

Definition: Physical Fitness Test

Example: We have a P.F.T. today.

Word: crater

Definition: Hit the ground

Example: 'I fell and almost cratered.'

Word: open-book

Definition: A place in a rock from 0 degrees to 150 degrees.

Example: 'The open-book had some interesting moves.'

Word: ruster-tail

Definition: The tail of water made when skiing.

Example: I was ripping and made some ruster-tails.

(Y.A., N.A., T.P., A.A., R.S., and B.K.)

Let's here it for the Summer of 2005 English 101 and 205 students! (sound of applause…)

Stay tuned for Part II in September, where I will be offer some linguistical delights from Science and Speculative Fiction world builders. Just to give you a little taste, here are a few from Boort, one of my multi-faceted fictional projects:

Word: Sozar (So-zharr)

Definitions: 1. an expletive like "awesome"; 2. a swear word (depending upon tone); 3. said as a toast and/or to congratulate someone; and 4. something said in frustration.

Examples:
"Sozar! I can't seem to find the portal to return home to Boort."

"The Boortian Ambassador just hired you as her personal assistant? Sozar to you!"

Word: Poochi Bug

Definitions: A type of honey-making "insect" (for want of a better category) that flies but can also maneuver on—and in—the ground. Their tiered hives can range in height from a few feet to over twenty-feet. Circumferences range in size as well. It is believed that certain types of Poochi Bugs burrow deep into the ground as well. They are considered to be poisonous to most humanoid species. The Poochi Bug and its behavior is a rich source of metaphor in the Boortian language group.

Examples:

"I wouldn't go out tonight if I were you…The Poochi Bugs are too quiet."

"Please join me for an aperitif—it's made with the finest Poochi Bug honey."

“Those Terrans have much to learn about our style of transgalactic trade negotiating. They’re larval at best.” (This is reference to Poochi Bug larvae. Just prior to hatching, they wriggle out of the hive, thus leaving themselves susceptible to other predators such as the Mora Blossom. The Mora Blossom is a plant know for its exquisite fragrance; it exists in a symbiotic relationship with the Mora Spider, another deadly creature. Interesting to note, however, is that the Mora Spider’s venom has psychotropic properties. There is also a belief that individuals with the appropriate genetic codes are capable of transdimensional travel once bitten.)

“You really need a vacation...You look like you’ve been building hives.” (This is a reference to the Poochi Bug Hives which are constructed much like a village. It also references the underground activities of certain clandestine movements engaged in transgalactic political schemes.)

In closing, here’s a little poem of mine dedicated to the to the writers and enforcers of the "Extra-Terrestrial Exposure Law—Part I". May you be exposed to aliens!

Exposed to Aliens

I've been exposed to aliens,
but I'm not going to tell D.C.,
‘cause they would fine and
imprison me, arbitrarily.

Hey—I thought that NASA
was on the extra-terrestrial's side,
but it's all just a cover-up,
an unwelcome compromise.

Those prisons are not for criminals,
like druggies, thieves or muggers;
they're for us, the contactees,
or are we now the contactors?

No matter how you play it,
tic-tac-toe—you lost!
How could we have been so stupid,

our common sense was tossed.

They plan to lock us up,
then throw away the key,
probe our minds and bodies
for secrets and disease.

But we'll show them, won't we,
who's really in charge of things,
as we beam their arses somewhere,
perhaps Pluto—or Saturn's rings.

It's hard being an alien...
What happened to "welcome to earth"?
It's really pissed us off some,
diffused our usual mirth…

But since we're rather reasonable,
and don't believe in giving in,
we'll stay on earth for the duration,
give your planet another spin.

Business Stuff:
You mean you can really make money with this?

Do what you love and the money will follow. . .
--Delonto Mae Kirk Relf,
the author's grandmother

Write everything like you're paid $1,000 per word.
--Charlene Baldridge, Writer and Mentor

Poets, the First Amendment, and Responsibility: Questions, Questions, and More Questions

I often hear people talk about the responsibility of poets, that it is their responsibility, in essence, to comment, through poetry, on major political and human rights issues, on disasters such as 9-11 and other global atrocities, and so forth.

Why is it their responsibility? Are poets the voice of the people? Are poets urban shaman who look into the body, mind, and spirit of a people, then share what they see? Are poets public servants who take a vow or sign a contract to take care of the people by writing poems to answer those difficult to answer questions, to give voice to unspoken/unutterable hopes and fears? Are poets supposed to create anodynes for pain? Soothe madness?

In some countries where free speech is limited, where poets are tortured, imprisoned, assassinated, is it a poet's responsibility if they live in a "free" country to speak for those who are unable?

Does a poet's particular "day job" dictate what type of poetry they should or should not hold up to the public view? Case in point, English teachers who write erotica. Enter pseudonyms, and while I've often been told that I should have published this or that poem under a pseudonym because colleagues think I'm too kinky or that the school where I work might call me into the office and scold me like a child (remember the old guidelines for teacher behavior—especially for women? We're not supposed to be sexual beings even if we're married!)

So, should a poet write about whatever they want? Do they have a moral obligation to anyone other than their own conscience?

I've heard all the above questions, complete with a library filled with commentary. Just as no one can definitively answer the questions: "what is poetry?"— "or what is a poem?"— it's difficult to pin down the above.

Don't poets have the freedom of choice to be any type of poet they want? Even a bad poet by those academic standards that so many are fond of pontificating?

Haven't you heard someone say "poets have to be honest"—or that they should be honest?

Have you heard someone complain about well-establish poets and criticize them for not writing about "serious" subjects? That they're having too much fun, and well, incidentally, they're superficial? Or that their poems are about violence or sappy pre-feminist subjects such as being in-love and being willing to do anything for the man or woman who is the object of their affection?

What of the poet who makes fun of someone's walk or speech? The way they eat? What of the poet who makes fun of governments, of "all the king's horses and all the king's men"? What of the poet who accuses their father of incest, their mother of neglect, their teacher for not educating them?

At what point in the causal chain does a poet enter "dangerous territory"? Is it their job, their purpose, their calling to do so? To shake it up, mix it up, defy social norms and taboos—even in language itself?

Or can poets "just" write for themselves? Is that selfish? Does it defy the purpose of poetry?

Poetry is writing, and as such, has multiple purposes: to inform, to persuade, or to entertain. I would add to arouse—emotion, passion, anger, and all those other emotions. Perhaps a poet's purpose is to inspire you to write, to speak, to think, to question, to answer, to discover, to sleep, to sing, to share and/or exchange knowledge, to impart wisdom, to show another way of "looking" at a situation.

What do you think a poet's purpose is?

How to Make a Living as a Poet: A List-With Updates!

Here are a few ways you can make a living as a poet:

- Teach poetry
- Facilitate poetry workshops
- Be a poetry coach
- Compile your poetry in a book-length manuscript and get it published
- Get your name on one of those "best-seller"
- Have regular speaking engagements and charge a lot of money
- Be a visiting poet at a prestigious university where they give you room, board, and a stipend for printer ribbons, postage, and paper
- Be a poet-in-the-schools
- Win major contests on a regular basis
- Sell your poetry to family, friends, and that English teacher who all said, "you're a good poet"
- Find a benefactor
- Get a grant
- Become a poet laureate

- Join with other poets to create an on-or-off-line publication where you charge big bucks for advertising
- Write greeting cards
- Write poetry-to-order
- Put your poetry to music and become a (insert favorite form of music here) star
- Climb into that time machine, travel back to the proverbial "good old days" when kings and queens had court poets
- Invest the money you earn from selling poetry so that your poems gain more interest
- Become a poetry marketing guru
- Learn how to accept rejection because it is a "numbers" game
- Put your poetry on T-shirts, coffee mugs, mouse pads, and all those other blank canvasses (I hope I don't need to tell you to do this yourself so that some organization who shall remain nameless doesn't profit from your work)
- Write articles about poetry and get them published
- Write reviews on poetry books and get them published
- Become a therapist and prescribe poetry writing
- Get a stand-up comic gig and include poetry in your schtick
- Be a bartender and offer to compose an on-the-spot poem for donations
- Barter your poetry coaching services and/or poems for meals, drinks, rent, and other essential wants and needs
- Open an online or brick-and-mortar bookstore that sells poetry books

I hope you don't think I'm being flippant. . .It's true that some of the above are more easily said than done, but manifesting what you need and want in your life begins with believing it is so. Who knows how far you can get? You may be the poet who alters the "profession" (and this is one of the oldest professions, in case you were wondering). But please, please, please don't quit your day—or night job—to **become** a poet. "Just" **be** a poet!

Here's a question for you: If you never made money as a poet, would you still write poetry? If you answered, "no", then I have to tell you that you may not be a poet. I hate to be the bearer of bad news, but if you're not compelled to write, if the Muse doesn't drag you kicking and screaming to your journal, your notebook, or your computer on a regular basis, then perhaps you may want to try fiction (note: the same rules apply here as well).

Get the picture?

Seriously, though, there's hope. You don't need to postpone this until vacation time or until you retire. Yes, you can write poetry and still hold down a "regular" job (whatever that is...) Well, some people can. For example, I teach part-time, have a freelance writing/editing/coaching business, and I get paid for some of what I write. In general, I only submit to paying publications and contests.

Yes, I've been paid for poetry. The most I've received for a single poem is about $30. The least, zero. Lots of zeros...(oh that they followed a double or triple-digit figure). But I'm not complaining. Really I'm not. Does this mean that I don't want to be paid for poetry, that it's some self-less, altruistic act?

Of course not. I can't even begin to tell you how selfish I am. How I fantasize about my poems-in-process as well as the ones I haven't yet met. So many poems—alas! So little time.

There's nothing like the winning of a "poem of the month" contest or that e-mail from an editor at another publication you admire saying, "we want it!" Another great rush is when someone comes up to you after a reading and says they love your stuff, or that you inspired them to start writing again. Then there's the awesome people who publish your first collection, the second, the third. . .

Who are you?
Some comments on writing the authorial bio

I was playing around with the idea of writing a column on bios when I received my May's writersdigest.com newsletter. I scrolled through James V. Smith Jr.'s prompts, taken from his *Fiction Writer's Brainstormer.* The one for May 31st reads as follows:

"Write your author bio. It's a resume of everything you've done as an author".

Come on, **everything**?

I don't think so.

The authorial bio, or just "bio", for short, is an excellent device to keep track of what you've done as well as where you're going. While writers have actual resumes and/or vitaes, the bio provides a little "taste".

While a bio (i.e., an abbreviation for "biography" in this context) is not an interview per se, it could potentially inspire someone to conduct an interview with you! By its nature, a bio asks for information about you, the writer. It is a synopsis of your life from birth to the present moment, or perhaps more succinctly, your life since you became—or realized—you were a writer. Does ones writerly life begin before or after publication? Hmmm. . .I wonder. I actually listed my very first publication in a few bios. I was six, and it was for a school publication. The zines got a kick out of it.

Bio lengths vary as do the guidelines for writing them. I've come across a few who don't include bios and others who only want bios if you've been accepted for publication. There's a trend, though, to ask for bios when you submit material. Wonder why this is. Could it be because they want to know if anyone else has published you yet? And if so, then who?

Many publications ask for a "short bio", but then don't define what that is. Some define, "short", as "no more than 50 words" or "no more than 100 words", while others state to "include a 3-sentence bio". Many writers can make those 3-sentences exceed 100 words, though!

Then there's the publications who request the "profes-sional" bio. (not that the other ones aren't professional. . .) Think "upscale journals", academic presses, etc. These publications are generally interested in the following: degrees you hold; where you "lecture"; courses you teach; nominations and awards; editorial boards upon which you've served, contests you've judged. That sort of thing.

Bios are a marketing tool, as they tell editors—and the universe at large—who you are, what you've done, what you're about to do, what you're planning to do, and so forth. They also say who you know, who likes you, who doesn't, and if you're getting paid.

Does that matter in this post-post-modern world?

You betcha!

In my own capacity as a poetry editor, I want to know about the people behind—or inside—the poems. I love reading about writers—period.

I loved British Literature in high school (remember that favorite English teacher of mine, Lynn Frank-Green?). One of the reasons I was fascinated by this body of work, and the class in general, was because our teacher told us the skinny on these writers.

One can't help wondering how the Ivory Tower was ever erected to house such deviants...Perhaps it is a sort of prison—but that's another column.

Something interesting to note is that many writers claim they don't like writing their own bios. Why? Are they part of the "author is dead" camp, so they don't think it matters? Do they want to remain reclusive? Anonymous?

Do they wish they were someone else?

That's easy. Invent a new writing persona. The best way I've found for doing this is composing the third-person bio, which many publications prefer, by the way. Talking about your self in the third person can be liberating, because it may alleviate some of the pressure—and no, it does not cause split personality disorder...

Be sure to include your name—or nom de plume—and where you live (not your actual address, but something like, San Diego, California, US, or Earth, Milky Way Galaxy).

When you study the publications to which you plan to send your work (always a great idea), you'll develop a sense of what they like in a bio. Some don't want a list of your publications, while others seem to hold the view that "more is better". Many just want to know something intriguing about you, like Cathy Buburuz at Champagne Shivers (available at: http://www.samsdotpublishing.com). Tyree Campbell, the publisher of Samsdotpublishing.com, often pens bios based on what he knows—or thinks he knows—about his writers (he's always right on with me...Can't hide anymore...).

Maybe you can start a business writing bios for people who don't feel like writing their own. You could also start a collection of bio poems about yourself and other people. I have a collection in process, *My Friend, the Poet, and other poems about people I think I know* (more shameless self-promotion prior to publication). The possibilities are endless.

I've decided to include a few of my bios just to give you an idea of context as well as theme and variation.

This one was sent to a "professional" publication:

"Terrie Leigh Relf teaches English at San Diego City College. In addition to serving on the editorial board of *City Works (*City College's literary arts journal), Relf is the poetry editor and "Poet's Workshop" columnist for http://www.WritersMonthly.US, pens "The Mistress of Rhetoric" column for *The Espresso*, San Diego's coffee and cafe culture newspaper, and has recently returned to http://www.visionmagazine.com. An internationally published writer, publication highlights include: *Flashshots, Fifth Dimension, The Martian Wave, Aoife's Kiss, Between Kisses, GuillermoBosch's Saucebox, Manifold, Nightingale, WritersHood, Writeronline, Sol-magazine, Moxie magazine, Sex and the Single Alien* et al.

Upcoming publications include *NFG, Underworlds, Wondrous Web Worlds III*, and *Unspeakable Limericks."*

This one was send to a publication that handles SF and spec poetry and fiction:

"Her articles, fiction, and poetry have appeared extensively both on and off-line. Recent publications include *Vision Magazine, Flashshots, EOTU, Muse Apprentice Guild, Word Master, WriterOnline, Absolute Write, Wondrous Web Worlds 3, Nightingale, Aoife's Kiss, The Fifth Dimension, Martian Wave, Sol-Magazine, Buddha's Temple, Lucy Westenra, The World Haiku Review* and *Writers Hood.*

Her second collection of poetry, *Metro Madness and other poems,* is now available through Lucy Westenra ebooks at: http://toadmama_pooh.tripod.com/bloodletterspressandelfhelperinc/index.html."

This one was sent this one to Lucian Dragos at http://www.wordmaster.ev.ro./
(NOTE: He sent it back and asked for a personal one):

"Terrie Leigh Relf lives in San Diego, CA, USA. She is the poetry editor and "Poet's Workshop" columnist for http://www.WritersMonthly.US, pens "The Mistress of Rhetoric" column for *The Espresso*, and has recently returned to *Vision Magazine* as a staff writer and editor. When Relf isn't writing, she teaches English Composition and Critical Thinking at San Diego City College, volunteers for San Diego Writers Co-op, participates in several on-line writing and critique groups, coaches private writing clients, and runs a freelance writing and editing business.

An award winning and internationally published writer, her work has also appeared in *Sol-Magazine, The WritersHood, The Martian Wave, Fifth Dimension, Aoife's Kiss, Sex and the Single Alien, Lucy Westenra, Blood Dreaming, Guillermo-bosch's Saucebox, The T.S. Eliot Hypertext Poetry Project, Moxie Magazine, Nightingale, Manifold, Flashshot, the World Haiku Review, Buddha's Temple, Haiku Harvest, Starfish, Amaze Cinquain Journal,* and others. Her chapbook, *Lap Danced by the Muse,* was released last fall by WritersMonthly.US.

Upcoming publications include *Flashshot, NFG, Underworlds,* and *Wondrous Web Worlds III.* Lucy Westenra Press will be releasing a collection of her horror and speculative poetry, *Metro Madness and Other Poems,* sometime this year."

I recently had the honor to serve as one of the judges for the African American Writers and Artists Organization's literary arts competition. This is what I sent them:

"Terrie Leigh Relf is the poetry editor and "Poet's Workshop" columnist for writersmonthly.us. She also pens the "Mistress of Rhetoric" column for The Espresso. Relf teaches writing at San

Diego City College, where she has served on the editorial staff of *City Works. S*he's also been a preliminary judge for several local competitions—including a slam or two.

An award winning and internationally published poet, Relf's recent and upcoming publications include *Sidereality, Aoife's Kiss, Fifth Dimension, Underworlds, Muse Apprentice Guild, Sol-magazine, Vision Magazine, Eotu,* and *Poetry Super Highway.* Her second collection of poetry, *Metro Madness and other poems* has just been released by Lucy Westenra e-books. Her third collection, *Jupiter's Eye,* will be released sometime this fall."

Since, I'm also a fiction writer. Here are a few that I submitted with my flash fiction pieces to *Flashshot, Daily Genre Flash Fiction* (available at: http://flashshot.tripod.com/):

"Terrie Leigh Relf lives in San Diego, CA, where she warps minds in a local community college English Department. Her work has appeared extensively both on and offline. Upcoming publications include the Samsdot anthology, *Outposts of Beyond."*

Here's another one:

"Spend some time with Terrie Leigh Relf, and you may decide she's a bit strange. Students often run for the door when they encounter her bizarre sense of humor. Her fiction is often based on the multiple realities she inhabits as well as on people she "knows"—so watch out!"

This one is for an anthology of scifaiku, *Random Planets,* from Samsdotpublishing.com. The publisher, Tyree Campbell, who has a highly developed sense of humor, has probably "tinkered" with it a bit. But maybe not. It's due in the mail any day now…

"About six years ago, Terrie Leigh Relf bought her first home computer. Once she was online, the first thing she looked for was haiku sites. Lo and behold, Tom Brinck's scifiku site came up. Needless to say, she was ecstatic. A place where her two major loves came together? Life on earth has not been the same since...Through the scifikulistserve, she met Oino Sakai, Teri Sanitoro, Viki Tarrani, Andree Gendron, and several other fine scifikujin. Through the fine tutelage of these people, she learned how to write scifaiku. Her first scifaiku appeared in Oino Sakai's Starleaper. Then, Andree Gendron and Teri Sanitoro told her about Promartian...The rest is history." [I did *not* tinker with this. It was on my "to tinker with" list, but I forgot. TC]

This one I submitted with a flash fiction piece, "Bathland", to *EOTU's* August issue (available at: http://www.clamcity.com/eotu.html). Please cross your appendages for me. . .

"Terrie Leigh Relf lives in San Diego, CA. Sometimes, she wishes she lived elsewhere. An island perhaps, with no distractions save the gentle swell of warm water. . .

Upcoming fiction publications include *5th Dimension* and *Outposts of Beyond.* Her newest collection of poetry, *Metro Madness and other poems*, has just been released from Lucy Westenra Ebooks."

That's enough about me. . .

The next time you're asked to send in a bio, ask yourself how you want the universe to "read" you—or ponder who the editors want you to be. . .There's a subtle, but profound, difference.

Some Thoughts as to Whether or Not Sim-Subbing is Such a Good Idea

What, you may ask, is a "sim", and how does, or would, one sub or not sub it?

If this were one of those "word association" tests, some people might immediately think of a simulated human being, or as they are referred to in some quadrants, synthetic humans (AKA Synths). Androids, robots, cyborgs, and a veritable cornucopia or additional beings may also come to mind. Another person, perhaps one with a military background or prone to reading—or viewing—a variety of genres might begin to visualize a some sort of submarine releasing a small—or smaller—pod into the water. Still others may consider the word, "simulacra", and begin to have nightmares that they're still in grad school, and surrounded by postmodern theorists expounding mutually exclusive, and yet strangely similar positions on the existence and/or the nonexistence of the author.

Of course all of the above is just a bit of fun, you and I both know that a "simsub" is a "simultaneous submission". Well, at least I now know...When I first began to focus on really getting published (as opposed to just simulating the action, i.e., actually sending work out), I had no idea what it meant. I was pretty darn embarrassed, too, when someone explained it to me like I was some kind of neophyte or something, which I was, but jeez, did they have to make so much fun of me?

To add further embarrassment to the situation, after this well-meaning friend explained what simsubbing was, I expressed genuine confusion. Why would someone send the same poem, story, or article out to multiple publications?

After the laughter died down again, my friend said something like: "your chances of getting that piece picked up at all—if any—of those publications is about nil. And if it does happen, then you decide which publication is more reputable, which one pays better, and so forth, then send a 'thanks but no thanks' letter."

That didn't set well with me then, and I admit to it still not sitting well with me now. Still, I know quite a few people who do engage in this practice, and the law of averages actually does seem to apply. The only time I've done this myself has been an accident (Yes, I admit to occasionally keeping ah-er-ah, bad, I mean, incomplete, records…)

While many publishers and/or editors will say, "Don't do it!" there are others who will say: "If you do it, don't tell us". I've actually seen a few writers guidelines that address it with a "we know you're going to do it, so the least you can do is let us know if it's accepted elsewhere." And yes, there are those who say "ok, go ahead", as if it's expected. I actually know a few who will put you on a very special list if they discover you've simsubbed.

Trust me- - -You don't want to be on that list.

As always, there are variations on this theme, so why the hoopla?

Well, there are several obvious reasons, and a few that may not be as obvious. Consider the following gleaned from a few sources who preferred remaining anonymous (NOTE: I've taken the liberty of embellishing for entertainment value.):

1. If you didn't intend it for us then why did you send it to us?
2. What? You're pulling that poem I love most of all, the poem that I was going to publish, the poem that is already mocked-up and ready-for-print? How could you?!
3. This is the third time you've done this. . .Please don't do it again.
4. It's already gone-to-print—and no, we're not going to yank the run unless you're footing the bill!
5. We thought you liked us. Please tell us that this was accidental, that you really didn't intend to create all this EXTRA WORK for us…

Why don't I simsub? For one, I like to keep things moving. When I first began to submit my work, I would send out a poem or a short story, wait for weeks, sometimes months, for a response. It's not that I didn't write during these extended waiting periods, but I didn't send out much else.

I don't remember when it finally dawned on me. No doubt one of my many mentors took me aside, told me to "keep it flowing!"

At this writing, I'm waiting to hear back on two "essays", eighteen short stories, and nineteen poems. There may be a few more I've missed (That record thing again. . .) I write, edit, and revise every day, so there's always something to send out (especially all those rejections.) I keep it fluid (It helps being a water sign. . .). There are times when I kick myself for sending something to one publication when it might be a better fit for another, but if it's accepted, I rejoice just the same. After all, even though I write because I love and need to write, I also do it to get published.

As an editor, I don't want simsubs for the some of the reasons cited above. Ok, for all the reasons cited above. Perhaps a solution for those who can't fight the urge to simsub is to focus on creating several ready-to-mail-out poems, short stories, articles, novels, and screen plays at a time. I'm sure that this is nothing new to you, but the more work you have in orbit, the better odds you have for pinging a landing dock.

Another point that bears repeating is that when a publication doesn't mention simsubs, it's not necessarily a green light to do so. I know I want to get in good with editors. I want them to like me. I want them to need me. I want to know what makes them happy because happy editors can really make a poet's–or any other type of writer's— life that much better.

When you get-in-good with editors, they may not only publish you–but hire you to be an editor, too.

Then you get to say: "ABSOLUTELY NO SIMSUBS!" With your award-winning smile. . .

Psst! Wanna know the Secret of Getting Published?

Just do it! (Sound of two fingers snapping)

It's truly amazing how simple it is to get published (sound of writer scrabbling for cover).

Seriously, though, once you've decided to get published, that's what happens. You get published. It's about focused intention; ok, and learning to read—and follow—those submission guidelines. . .and networking. . .and accepting rejection. . .and. . .and. . .and. . .

There's really nothing mystical or supernatural about the submission and publication process (Unless you're a medium and/or a channel for dead writers). Over the years, though, I've learned that in addition to making conscious decisions to "get published", being persistent, and all those other directives, that it's a willingness to edit and revise that has often been a determining factor.

It's simple, really (sound of paper shredder jamming). When a poem, short story, article—or whatever else you send out—comes back to you (a euphemism for "rejected"), take an honest look at it. Does it need editing? Revision? Did you send it to be "best" market possible? There's a good possibility that it may benefit from revision. (If not, then sound it out again without delay!)

First of all, writing is all about revision. It takes time, focus, and yes, desire. While many writers claim their process is nonlinear, others will say that they revise as they write, moving from the beginning, through the middle, then on to the end. I know writers who revise their work two-to-three times, and others who do so twenty-to-thirty times. On rare occasions, the first draft, with a bit of tweaking here and there, will "work". There really is no magic number, but if you want to create one, go ahead

Secondly, glossaries, dictionaries, thesauri, reference books, and online resources are essential tools. Read them daily. Become informed on standard, archaic, and alternate usage. Develop an awareness of the sounds of the words, the feelings, sensations, and thoughts that they invoke. A few strategically enhanced word choices can really make a difference.

Third, don't abandon a piece that's not working at the moment—and don't literally shred it out of existence. (I confess to doing both.) If a piece isn't working, put it to the side for awhile. If you're in the revision stage, save each draft, label accordingly, then keep revising. Create an "ideas" folder with the bits and pieces. Sometimes, all it takes is a phrase or two to seed a new piece. I've been known to transfuse between pieces, to "collage" them together.

Fourth, what is your intention? Who is your audience? What do you want your readers to see, hear, feel, taste, touch, or think? Where do you want to take them? What do you want to leave them pondering? While writing can be (and often is) about personal expression, catharsis, and all that, the chances are that you still want to share your work with others.

Fifth (yet another controversial issue), you "need" to read the work of other writers, if for no other reason than to see what they're doing. Who do you like? What is it that you like about their work? What does that work "do" for you? Examine this closely through modeling.

Sixth, learn about the craft through reading, discussing and workshopping. Find a mentor. Join on-line lists. Go to readings and other literary events. Read your own work in public. Writing is a developable skill; although some believe it's a gift bestowed by Calliope (Muse of Epic Song), Euterpe (Muse of Lyric Song), Thalia (Muse of Comedy and Bucolic Poetry) Erato (Muse of Erotic Poetry), or Polyhymnia (Muse of Sacred Song)five of Zeus and Mnemosyne's nine daughters. (available at:
http://ancienthistory.about.com/library/bl/bl_musepages.
htm?terms=The+Muses)

Seventh, when you're ready to submit your work for publication, follow the guidelines to the letter. If you're not familiar with the publication, be sure to read a few issues before you submit. This will save you (and yes, the editors) time and energy. Develop positive relationships with the editors of favorite publications. Careers have been made with the mentorship of a single publication…

The important thing is to keep writing. When your work is criticized, listen (unless they're really being nasty, then walk away). Remember it's "just their opinion"—informed or otherwise. When critiquing others, be kind, but honest. Critique as you would like to be critiqued.

Writing and Publishing Made Smarter—
NOT Harder!

Remember that college motto: "Study smarter, NOT harder"? Well, you don't need to be in college to continue chanting this mantra! In the proverbial long run, one of the purposes of school is to learn how to learn, right?

How does this apply to writing?

Well, here are a few "lessons" that may apply to your writing and publishing practices:

1. Be brave and get your work out there. As I've said over and over and over again, it's nice to stockpile for the future, but consider the possibility that the future is NOW.
2. Remember that if you make mistakes, so long as you learn from them, they're lessons;
3. Visit the WOL archives to read, "Some Thoughts as to Whether or Not Sim-Subbing is a Good Idea" and "Psst! Wanna know the Secret of Getting Published?" and "The Poetry Scam". Studying your makets, following editorial guidelines, being forewarned about real and imagined scams, as well as checking out the proverbial "rumour mill" of dastardly deeds and unethical practices is certainly putting you ahead of the game.
4. Still in the archives? Good. Read EVERYTHING there…Archives are an incredible treasure trove of vast resources. Besides, everything at WOL is good…
5. Did I mention that it's important to "toot your own horn"? While considered to be "shameless self-promotion" in some circles, it's actually termed "public relations" and shows that you believe in your self. It's also important to know how to hawk your wares.

6. Another strategy that I often employ is called "transfusion". I call it this because of the reference to blood (and you all know I'm also a horror writer, right?), the vital essence of life. Our ideas, thoughts, words, etc., are our vital essence as well. If a poem's not working, transfuse it into a piece of flash fiction or a longer story. If a short story isn't working because it's heavy on dialogue (I recently had a short story rejected for this very reason. The editor asked me if I was a scriptwriter!), then why not transfuse it into a feature-length script (NOTE: Be sure to read Christina Hamlett's articles in archives).
7. Read, read, read, and read some more. Read books and magazines and newspapers and online zines—and WOL regularly. Read what you write. Read what you want to write. Read about writing and reading. Repeat as necessary. What am I reading right now? Let's see…I just finished reading the *The Tower At Moorkai: Book Three of The Thran Chronicles* by H. David Blalock (available through http://www.booklocker.com. I'm rereading *The 2005 Rhysling Anthology: The Best Science Fiction, Fantasy, & Horror Poetry of 2004* (available through The Science Fiction Poetry Association, http://www.sfpoetry.com), and I'm about to dive into *The Code Book: How To MakeIit, Break It, HackIit, Crack It* by Simon Singh (available through Delacorte Press).
8. Set long-term, short-term and immediate writing and publishing goals. For example, one of my long-term goals is to have consecutive seven-figure book deals. One of my short-term goals is to "finish" *Blood Journey*, the novel I'm co-authoring with Henry Lewis Sanders, and to get it published (okay, that's two short-term goals, but they're definitely connected.) One of my immediate goals is to complete this article by deadline.
9. Join with other writers to workshop, network, and otherwise provide a support system for your writing and publishing process. As a college English instructor, I stress group work (much to most of my students' chagrin). One of the reasons I encourage—and require this—is due to the collaborative nature of the writing process.
10. Get out of your comfort zone! In order to develop as a writer (insert whatever that means to you), I think it's vital to push ourselves to the limit—and then push ourselves some more. Sometimes, this means trying on a new writing

hat (i.e., you want to be a famous poet, but hey, people like your articles, so focus on those, too), while other times it may mean increasing your writing practice time from three hours per day to five. Another method is to take a class (i.e., check out the WOL offerings) so that you're working with others who are also interested in expanding their writing experiences. This way, you have several people nudging you—including the course facilitator!

The Poetry Scam

I can't tell you how often I still hear about poets—and other writers—falling prey to publishing scams. While these are euphemistically known as "vanity presses" as well as other words and phrases that I won't list here, to borrow Gertrude Stein's rhetoric: a scam is a scam is a scam. Not only are you being cheated out of your hard-earned money, you are being cheated in other ways as well—being published in a legitimate venue.

As the former "Poet's Workshop" columnist for writersmonthly.us (now *WORD/San Diego*), I often included a Q&A section to address issues raised by readers and other writers I know. I've included one such Q&A for this issue of WOL, because I had several recent dialogues on just this issue.

Q: I've heard that there are a lot of poetry scams out there. Could you please fill me in?

A: Yes, there are quite a few poetry scams out there, "publishers" who prey on new and eager poets, as well as those who manage to hoodwink the more experienced. The first such publisher that comes to mind is poetry.com, perhaps because they're one of the more visible entities…

I put a request out to a few lists and groups with which I'm involved, and here's what they had to say:

"This is a trap—poetry.com. Years ago I fell for it and they published one of my poems. Somehow it got back into their system, only by now my name has changed; they published it even though I told them explicitly not to do so. Apparently, another one of my little ghoulish poems made another book, even though I have not returned the permission card at all. If you enter, you will be published; then, they will sell you the book for what is probably close to $100.00 now; I don't know for sure.

They do this for photography as well. I have one in one of their books, my niece has another. Total scam." (anonymous poet/artist)

Cathy Buburuz, Editor for *Champagne Shivers*, sent this in

response to my call for commentary:

"Cyberspace and mail boxes all over the world have been invaded by poetry scams disguised as contests with no entry fees. After you enter, you'll receive a letter telling you that your poem has been selected for a gorgeous leather-bound volume and for just a couple of hundred dollars, you can have your bio inserted and a copy delivered to your door. Then there's the scam whereby your acceptance letter states that you have been selected as a top poet, and for the bargain price of $50 or $60 you can have an engraved plaque that announces your talents as a poet. Then there's the one where you're expected to spend several hundred dollars to attend a poets' conference where you'll be presented an award and have a chance at thousands of dollars in prizes. Beware. Whenever a publisher asks a writer to part with their hard-earned dollars, it's a scam. The best advice I can give a new poet is never pay a contest fee and never send money to a publisher for anything. Do not submit to these leeches. Send your work to only those editors or publishers who offer payment (and at least one contributor's copy) for accepted work."

But rather than my going on and on, why not visit the following sites for more information?

No one can compare to Angela Adair Hoy and her team when it comes to publicizing those who take advantage of writers—whether it be for non-payment, false advertising, or just general bad manners…Thank you, Angela! You are a shining light!

Visit her "Whispers and Warnings" section for updates. Be sure to subscribe to her free newsletter, too.
http://www.writersweekly.com

The Science Fiction and Fantasy Writers of America, Inc. has a "writer alerts" section at their site:
http://www.sfwa.org/beware/

Duran Imboden, of writing.org, has a good article on poetry scams. It's available at:
http://www.writing.org/html/a_poetry_scams.htm

Visit another one of my favorite sites, absolutewrite.com. "Getting the Scoop on Poetry Contest Scams" by Gloriana is a good read. Check it out at:
http://www.absolutewrite.com/specialty_writing/poetry_scams.htm

What Editors Want and More Publishing Tips

Many people think that editors exist as a human equivalent to spell and grammar check, and in some cases, that is their "job".

In most cases, however, an editor's "job" is to read manuscripts for consideration in their respective publication. In some instances, they are a managing editor, which signifies that they have the last word as to whether or not a manuscript, be it a poem, an article, a short story, or a novel, will be published.

Sometimes, there is an acting editor, a person who may not have the final word, but close to it. . .These editors, along with their managing editors, shape content. They determine the mission of the publication, and work not only toward managing that vision, but maintaining and enhancing it. Sometimes, however, the submissions (AKA the slush pile) will dictate trends, themes, and so forth.

Then there is the next category of editor. . .These editors, who often work in teams, read manuscripts, move them from the "slush" pile to the "reject" pile, from slush to "still considering", or from slush to still considering to the "let's send this up the proverbial ladder" pile. It can be a very time-consuming process.

There are, of course, variations on the above, but managing editors, acting editors and team editors are the most obvious and the most prevalent. Or are they? Isn't it the readers—and their collective responses—who ultimately choose? How? By purchasing—and reading—the publications. . .

Advertisers and sponsors are another discussion. . .

So, how does one boost their publication credits? Consider these ten easy steps in non-hierarchical order.

- Regularly visit market lists, many of which are free, to determine which publications are open to submissions, which are closed, and so forth (e.g., Ralan.com).
- Subscribe to writing newsletters (e.g., writersdigest.com).
- Study the publications within which you'd like to see your work. Subscribe, or purchase a sample copy, so that you know your work suits their wants and/or needs.
- Read the guidelines carefully; they are there for a reason, and reflect what a publication both wants and needs (and also what they do not want and do not need). Follow them to the letter.
- If a publication—or publisher—wants a query first, then query; don't send the entire manuscript unless they ask for it.

- Don't trust spell or grammar check. Proofread your work thoroughly for mechanical and other types of errors of commission or omission.
- If you include outside sources within your work, be sure that you cite them appropriately; otherwise, it's plagiarism.
- Join an on-or-off-line writing group (e.g., Critters.org), and otherwise connect with writers on a regular basis for networking, workshopping, and so forth.
- Read what other people are doing; no one writes in a vacuum.
- Attend writing workshops, conferences, and other "writerly" events.

Remember that editors, in many cases, are also writers—and people, too. Many of them wear a variety of hats, and if a positive relationship is cultivated with them, careers—and not just a few credits—may be born.

Performance Poets – Taking Poetry From the Page to the Stage

While many poets claim to write for the page and publication, others have the urge to get up on that stage and perform their poetry.

Some poets do both—and regularly. While the adage, "poetry is meant to be shared", often applies, whether or not someone chooses to read in public may just be a personal preference. There is, of course, the usual peer pressure, and encouragement, to perform by like-minded individuals.

Taking the Stage

If you're one of those people who wants to be on stage, but aren't sure if you're ready yet, remember that everyone starts somewhere—whether it's in front of a creative writing class, a peer review group, or at a local cafe.

It's true that some poets seem to own the stage from the moment that mic is in their hands. While they may be "naturals" and resonate with magnetic energy, chances are that they have practiced their work over and over and over again. They may even have had drama classes or already be an actor.

Develop Audience Awareness

When you know that you'll be reading your work in public, it may alter what--and how--you write it. While this has to do with formatting, line lengths, and other reading cues, it may also pertain to the style and genre of poetry. This situation is quite obvious if you've attended poetry readings and focused on the reader/audience dynamic.

There is no limit to what can be read--or performed--in public . .confessional poetry, political rants, humorous bits about love and other human emotions are all there. What response do these elicit? Anything from total silence to clapping to standing ovations with hoots and cat calls and raucous laughter.

Context is, as the saying goes, everything. If you're reading contemplative poetry to an audience that prefers spoken word with an edge, it may not go over that well. Then again, it might, as many poets write in a variety of venues, and the same poet who can call thunder from the skies can also be as still as the moon lingering over the ocean.

Develop Stage Presence

If you believe you've found the right venue for your work, but are waiting to "feel more comfortable" with the regulars, take the leap. Being comfortable on stage is usually something that's developed over time--and with frequency. After the first time you take the stage, you may even wonder what took you so long.

Here are a few tips and performance techniques this poet has collected over fifteen years of reading in public and being an emcee.

- Attend readings and observe how other poets read;
- Practice reading your poems—and record yourself;
- Experiment with different types of reading styles;
- Take speech and/or acting classes;
- Read your favorite poets aloud;
- Label negative thoughts "thinking"—you CAN do it!;
- Video tape yourself reading from the comfort of your home;
- Visualize yourself up there reading…hear the applause!;
- Start off by reading to friends who support you, then move up to reading in front of an open mic audience;
- Remind yourself of how much you love to write poetry, and that sharing your work with others is not only a great gift, but you may inspire others along the way.

So yes, performing in public does become more familiar, and as a result, easier. Focus on learning something from every reading--even if it's to take out a comma and change a word or two so that it flows better. Public readings also aid in the revision process, so if your audience doesn't respond the way you intended, give that some thought before reading that poem or poems again. Above all, believe in yourself and your work, be grateful to your audience, and who knows, you may even become an open mic emcee yourself.

And don't forget to breathe!

Organizational Tips and Time Saving Strategies

Writers are busy people, and just like other dedicated professionals, they are interested in creating more hours in the day.

While burning the proverbial candle at both ends may be a life-style choice, it doesn't mean that writers aren't in constant pursuit of effective organizational methods and time-saving strategies to manage their writing practice and careers. This is especially so, perhaps, with free-lance writers who also hold down non-writing day jobs, or writers who engage in a variety of projects simultaneously.

This method can be used by student writers, writers just starting out, as well as experienced writers with major deadlines. All you need to get started is a word processing program with folder icons.

Setting up Your Writing File Management System

At the beginning--or ahead of--each month, create and label a folder with the month, the year, and the file's purpose or function. Keep the titles simple and composed in language that works best for you, and modify--or otherwise add--additional folders to meet your needs.

Here is an assortment of file titles that this writer uses. By the end of the month, some of these will be full, while others may be empty or only have a few documents inside.

- 2010 May Acceptances
- 2010 May Correspondence
- 2010 May Deadlines
- 2010 May Miscellaneous
- 2010 May Newsletters to Read
- 2010 May Places to Submit
- 2010 May Rejections

- 2010 May Submissions
- 2010 May Work-in-Process

While the above categories' functions may seem obvious, which is intended, once you've used the method for awhile, you may notice that the category titles need modifying. You may need to include subfolders within the "work-in-process" folder, for example, if you regularly submit to a particular publication. Or, if you don't receive a lot of newsletters, you may want to just have a single newsletter folder to streamline your number of monthly folders. Keeping it simple--and personally relevant--is important on a time management level, as it cuts down on the time sifting through documents to locate work.

Managing Monthly Writing Folders

When you begin working with this system, transfer your work-in-process to its respective file, as this is an excellent place to get started. Also transfer other existing files to their folders (e.g., recent emails of acceptance, acknowledgment of receipt, etc.). Be sure, too, to appropriately label your documents--and their respective revision updates--accordingly, so that you're not spending time trying to figure out which is the most recent draft, etc. (e.g., on the road to Valhalla by Terrie Leigh Relf updated 1 May 2010).

While clicking on a file does provide the most recent date and time accessed, placing it in the file's title as well assists with eliminating confusion. Furthermore, it provides a document history just in case an earlier draft contains information that you may have eliminated. Be sure to save every five minutes or so and back up your files on a flash drive or another system (.e.g., emailing them to a web-based email account such as google).

How the System Works – an Anecdotal Account

It's Saturday, and you're determined to submit those poems you've worked so hard to revise. Once you've finished drafting the email to the editor and attaching or enclosing the poem(s), you include a Bcc on your email. Once the email is sent out and you receive the copy, save it to the "2010 May Submissions" folder along with the document file containing the poems.

Now that you've completed that task, you may be wondering what to do with all those drafts. One way to handle them is to just move them to the "2010 May Submissions" folder. Another way is to create a subfolder, which you label with the name of the publication to which you submitted them, the poems' titles, and the date of submission; then, all the material associated with that submission is in one place.

Watch Your Publication Credits Multiply

Since this system can assist you with organization and time management, you'll create more time to write and submit your writing. It's also a good method to keep a running tab on how much work you've submitted, how much has been accepted, rejected, etc. Be sure to turn around your rejections as soon as possible, and if there's a month when your rejections seem to outnumber your acceptances, revisit those folders full of acceptances--or encouraging remarks from editors!

Banned Books Week, September 2010

Banned Books Week will be celebrated in September on school campuses, at libraries, in bookstores, and at other public and private venues.

While September 24 through October 2, 2010, is the official week to promote awareness of banned and challenged books, events that occur during this week have the potential to resonate throughout the entire month and year as well as through entire generations of readers.

The First Amendment and the Freedom to Read

While intellectual freedom, free-speech, and the right to read whatever one wants may be perceived as a given within these United States, these rights are often challenged by public as well as private entities. While this, too, is a sign of democratic process, challenging the challengers is as well.

According to FindLaw.com, the First Amendment is as follows: "Congress shall make no law respecting an establishment of religion, or prohibiting the free exercise thereof; or abridging the freedom of speech, or of the press; or the right of the people peaceably to assemble, and to petition the Government for a redress of grievances." While there are other amendments that overlap the network of issues relating to banned books (e.g., the Fourth Amendment), this one is referred to on a regular basis.

Why Books are Banned and Challenged

There are probably as many reasons for banning and/or challenging the existence of any one book or series of books as there are individuals and groups who challenge them. The major reasons, however, tend to gravitate toward content that challenges a person's or group's individual belief systems in the arenas of religion, politics, and sex.

While many individuals may react emotionally prior to thinking, which is understandable, there are other individuals who dedicate their time and effort to eliminating access to books and other printed materials that do not promote their own agenda.

A Short List of Books that have been Banned or Challenged

In addition to other exceptional resources, The American Library Association at ALA.org provides the "Top Ten" challenged books for each year. Challenges are reported to the Office for Intellectual Freedom, and out of the 460 books reported in 2009, the top ten include the following:

- *And Tango Makes Thre*e by Peter Parnell and Justin Richardson, which was challenged for reasons associated with homosexuality
- *Twillligh*t (series) by Stephanie Meyer, which was challenged due to being "Sexually Explicit, Religious Viewpoint, Unsuited to Age Group"
- *My Sister's Keepe*r by Jodi Picoult, which was challenged dues to "Sexism, Homosexuality, Sexually Explicit, Offensive Language, Religious Viewpoint, Unsuited to Age Group, Drugs, Suicide, Violence"

While these and other books are on "the lists", they are still being read, discussed, written about, and otherwise promoted. This is a positive, isn't it? A sign that no matter how hard some individuals work to thwart our individual freedoms, they continue to prevail. True, it may be difficult for some to obtain and read these books, but there are ways around that, aren't there? This reader, for example, remembers classroom texts with lines blacked out because the teacher, principal, or school district deemed the material inappropriate.

It was an easy fix. In some cases, students would go to the library; in others, to their parents, grandparents, or neighbors' book shelves. Being resourceful is definitely a "developable" skill.

How to Maintain and Promote Intellectual Freedom

Revel in your intellectual freedom by reading at least one challenged or banned book a month. Encourage others to do the same. Start a reading group to discuss these books. Write about and otherwise promote them.

Remember the books that inspired and energized you, that took you on an adventure, that opened up the universe. Remember the books that caused you to question your own belief systems, that introduced you to the beliefs of others. What books elicited powerful emotions? What impact did that have on your life? Remember them all – even those books that you didn't like or would never read again.

Now imagine that the right to read those books was taken from you. . .How do you feel about that?

Work Cited

"The Top ten most frequently challenged books of 2009." The American Library Association. ala.org. 4 Aug. 2010. Web.

"The First Amendment - The US Constitution." FindLaw.com. 4 Aug. 2010. Web.

Writers and the Need for Copyrighting and Trademarking

This article provides a brief introduction to copyright and trademark registration and includes additional resources.

For several years now, I have been focusing on world building for a series of science and speculative fiction stories, articles, and novels. While I don't worry about anyone stealing my byline and fictional company and product names, as what has been already published is copyrighted, I've realized that the time has come to explore exactly what these terms mean, and to determine whether or not I need to register for marketing purposes.

Basic Definition of a Copyright

A copyright symbol looks like this: ©. According to the *United States Patent and Trademark Office: An Agency of the Department of Commerce's* website section, "What Are Patents, Trademarks, Servicemarks, and Copyrights?", it "is a form of protection provided to the authors of 'original works of authorship' including literary, dramatic, musical, artistic, and certain other intellectual works, both published and unpublished. The 1976 Copyright Act generally gives the owner of copyright the exclusive right to reproduce the copyrighted work, to prepare derivative works, to distribute copies or phonorecords of the copyrighted work, to perform the copyrighted work publicly, or to display the copyrighted work publicly."

In order to register a work, or collections of works, visit the *Copyright Office of the Library of Congress* site at copyright.gov. Registration fees begin at $35, and vary depending upon the medium of what is being registered (e.g., text, photo, etc.), the number of items, as well as the manner in which they are registered (i.e., electronic or paper filing, etc.).

Basic Definition of a Trademark

The trademark symbol looks like this: ™, and is seen alongside a variety of product names. According to the *United States Patent and Trademark Office: An Agency of the Department of Commerce's* website FAQ section, a trademark is basically a brand name. The section states that it "includes any word, name, symbol, or device, or any combination, used, or intended to be used, in commerce to identify and distinguish the goods of one manufacturer or seller from goods manufactured or sold by others, and to indicate the source of the goods."

Basic Definition of a Service Mark

A service mark is the same as a trademark, according to uspto.gov, but the basic difference is that it indicates the source of services to be rendered. In other words, it refers to the company which provides those services.

Basic Definition of a Registered Trademark

A registered trademark looks like this: ®, and is seen alongside product names and other related materials. It basically signifies that a company has had their product federally registered.

Federal Laws and Registering Trademarks

While federal laws don't mandate that a trademark has to be registered, uspto.gov's FAQ section indicates that there are "several advantages, including notice to the public of the registrant's claim of ownership of the mark, a legal presumption of ownership nationwide, and the exclusive right to use the mark on or in connection with the goods or services set forth in the registration."

In order to register, visit the uspto.gov's site to begin. One of the features of this site is the "Trademarks Process" sidebar that takes you through it step-by-step. The site also provides Intellectual Property Right Laws and other pertinent information. From what I gathered from looking at the application, there is a filing fee of $325 for what they refer to as the Trademark Electronic Application System, or TEAS, form for a "class of goods and/or services." There is also a TEAS Plus form, which "has stricter filing requirements." The cost to file this form is $275.

State and Local Laws

In order to determine if a particular state or city requires trademark registration, it's important to contact the pertinent office or website. In California, for example, the Secretary of State is Deborah Bowen. Under the "Business Programs" section, there is a subsection titled "Trademarks and Servicemarks", that provides additional information. There is a brief statement about the role of the Secretary of State's office, which is that it "maintains registration and all updates of California state trademarks and service marks. This information is accessible to the public upon request. General provisions governing trademarks and service marks are found in the Model State Trademark Law, California Business and Professions Code sections14200 et seq."

In closing, it is definitely challenging to study the materials above in order to determine whether or not one needs to register fictional products and services. As in the case of epic films such as *Star Wars,* when products such as Battle Stars and droid dolls are created, it goes without saying that there are lawyers, agents, and other personnel who handle those aspects; the products are definitely registered in order to protect the rights of the creator.

But what of the writer that is just starting out and/or is beginning to gain some exposure? Given today's marketplace, it's vital to promote ones own work in addition to any promotional assistance from publishers--especially those who are associated with the small press. These issues definitely call for additional research, and this writer would definitely welcome additional tutelage until she can afford her own personal Intellectual Property Attorney!

Work Cited:

Copyright Office of the Library of Congress. copyright.gov. Web. 29 Aug. 2010.

"FAQ Section." *United States Patent and Trademark Office: An Agency of the Department of Commerce. uspto.gov. Web. 29 Aug. 2010.*

"Trademarks and Servicemarks." *Secretary of State Deborah Bowen. sos.ca.gov. Web. 29 Aug. 2010.*

"What Are Patents, Trademarks, Servicemarks, and Copyrights?" United States Patent and Trademark Office: An Agency of the Department of Commerce. uspto.gov. Web. 29 Aug. 2010.

The Bio: A Self-fulfilling Prophecy?

This piece was previously published online under "How to Write an Authorial Bio" at suite101.com on September 4, 2010.

Penning a bio to accompany a poetry, fiction, or article submission can be an excellent focusing tool, an excellent marketing strategy, as well as fun.

In a publication's submission guidelines, many editors will request that an authorial bio be included with the submission. Other editors may indicate that if a piece is accepted for publication, they will request it at that time. Still others may assume that a writer should know to include it – period. It is therefore important to read those guidelines very carefully, as there are even a few editors out there who will delete an entire submission if all the submission requirements aren't met. In general, however, editors are decent and patient human beings who care about assisting others with their submission process.

Bio Length: Short or Long?

Bio length is usually determined by the publication, or publisher, to which work is submitted. Many publishers will specify character or word length, while others may ask for one to three sentences or a paragraph or two. Since much depends on available space, an average bio may range in length from 150 to 300 words. If space is a major consideration, as with twitter-length bios for publications like Stephen Wilson's *Microcosms*, the bio cannot exceed 43 characters.

Point-of-View: First Person, Second Person, or Third Person?

First person bios, which make "I" statements, such as the following bio: "I am a poet, fiction writer, and writing coach living in Ocean Beach, CA." While this one could be, and has been, expanded upon, it does provide some information. Perhaps the most important bit of information here is that the author lives in Ocean Beach, and so it may serve as a connecting point for other poets, fiction writers, and writing coaches in Ocean Beach. Think: Networking.

Second person bios are not seen as often, but they are acceptable in many venues, and can be humorous or fun. As with fiction, it addresses the proverbial "you", and can potentially create a conversational tone. An example of this type of bio may read like this: You know that you're a purveyor of quirky poetry, so I would like to suggest you read my latest collection, *My Friend, the Poet, and poems about other people I think I know*, which was recently released from Sam's Dot Publishing. Who knows. . .You may recognize yourself in one of my poems."

Bios are most often seen in third person, which is considered to be more professional. Many writers confess that it's easier to write about themselves in the third person, though, and it can make the process "easier" as a result. Here is an example of this type of bio: "Terrie Leigh Relf is on staff at Sam's Dot Publishing where she edits *Hungur Magazine*, serves as the contest editor for *The Drabbler*, and serves on the Special Projects Committee."

Including Organizational Memberships

Some publications will request that a writer's organizational memberships are included within their bios. Even if they don't, it is good practice to include this, as many of these organizations, such as The Horror Writers Association and The Science Fiction Poetry Associations, have strict requirements, and it demonstrates that a writer has some experience with getting published.

Including Publication History

While some publications will clearly state that they don't want a list of credits, others will ask for them outright. This, like the organizations above, may point to a writer's level of professionalism and experience. For those writers who have pages of credits, it's important to edit that down to a more manageable list. This editor suggests most recent publications as well as those that have been accepted for, and/or are upcoming from, a given publication.

The Bio as Self-fulfilling Prophecy

If a writer isn't ready to send out their work yet, an excellent writing exercise is to pen a bio as if that work was "good-to-go". Another way to approach this exercise is to draft a bio as if one were already a well-known published writer listing their accolades. Put it aside for awhile, then return to it in a few months to a year, and it may resonate with truth.

In closing, it's also good practice to create a document file with a variety of bios so that when an editor asks for one, it's already on hand. Enjoy the process--and remember to write and submit something every day.

Nom de Plumes, Pen Names, and Aliases—Oh My! (Or Why Do I Need a Pen Name Anyway?)

This piece was previously published under the title "Why Pen Name?" online at suite101.com on October 7, 2010.

This article discusses why an author might want to use a pseudonym, nom de plume, or alias rather than their given name.

The world of writing is full of authors who choose not to use their given, or legal, name when submitting their work for publication. There are a variety of reasons for doing this, most of them arising from honest intentions.

Writers Who Cross Genres, or Genre-Crossing

If an author usually writes in one genre, such as horror, and they want to try their hand at another, such as science fiction, they may want to test the waters under a pseudonym. Why? It could be a test run to see if they can expand their readership. It could also be because they don't want to lose fans in one genre while they're exploring another. It basically boils down to the proverbial "ask the author", because their reasons do vary.

Writers Who Switch Genders, or Gender-Switching

There is a long tradition of women who write under male nom de plumes, such as George Sand and George Eliot, whose given names were Mary Ann Evans and Mme. Amandine Aurore Lucie Dupin, Baronne Dudevant, respectively. Once upon a time, this was a necessity in order to have ones work taken seriously and published. Another reason relates to the proverbial having a reputation to uphold.

Over the years, this author has met several male authors who write romance fiction under a female alias. Then there are writers who believe that they need to cross genders in order for their work to be taken seriously. A male author who generally writes strong female characters, or uses a female voice, may not want to be accused by militant Feminists of "co-opting"; the same may hold true for female writers who don't want to be accused of "selling out". Ultimately, the author's agent, editor, and/or publisher usually know the legal name of whom they're working with, but the readers may not. . .

Writers Who Collaborate, or Co-Authorship

When writers collaborate, some may choose to create a single name that represents them both. It may be to distinguish their collaborative work from their solo work. It may also be to create a persona, much like actors do, in order to step into a new style of writing. It may also be "just for fun" or to assist each other in gaining a readership. Consider the husband-wife team of Henry Kuttner and Catherine L. Moore who wrote quite a few stories and novels under the pseudonym, Lewis Padgett. One of these, "Mimsy were the Borogroves", made it to the silver screen a few years back as *The Last Mimsy.*

Writers Who Have Career Conflicts, or Day Job issues

When writers have day jobs, or careers, that may be in conflict with their subject matter, etc., they may choose to use an alias so as not to jeopardize their position or reputation at work. Consider a vampire erotica writer who teaches school. While K-12 teachers may experience more flack than a college or university level instructor, this writer experienced a considerable amount of criticism from colleagues at a community college for her early horror writings. In retrospect, I do not regret using my given name, but some writers who also teach may want to consider this as an option. It's possible that had I been writing scholarly articles about this subject matter, I would have been treated with more respect. Then again, given the climate of said community college, it is doubtful.

Why Do Writer's Use Pen Names?

Regardless of an author's rationale, it has recently come to my attention that in many cases, when a writer chooses to write--or publish--under a pseudonym, they become immediately suspect in some circles. Why is this? A writer is well within their rights to use a pen name, aren't they? What if they're using an alternate name, or alias, to prove a point? To showcase a new genre of work? To present themselves in a more positive light?

If a writer is using an alias to avoid legal sanctions, that is another topic all together.

Using Pen Names – Readers Respond

This piece was previously published online at suite101.com on November 2, 2010.

This is a continuation of "Why Use a Pen Name?" that includes commentary from readers as well as personal anecdotes.

Even though many writers profess the usual reasons for using pen names, it seems that there really is no one reason – and their rationale may shift with time.

Writers Who Work in Different Professions

One reader responded that she needed to use a pen name to protect her identity as she is often called into court as an expert forensic witness. It is a way to separate her professional life from her life outside that profession.

Writers Who Believe Their Surnames Create Barriers

Another reader responded that "sometimes the sad reality is that someone having an ethnic name won't ring well with possible buyers and is a bad marketing decision, and a pen name may be required in order to sell more books. I have considered this as I'm sure many people have."

The reverse also holds true. For example, I've met quite a few authors over the years who have asked me if they should use their maiden names, their mother's and/or father's surnames, as they (and I quote) "sound more ethnic." If a publishing house, contest drive, or other type of call for submissions wants Latin writers, then having a last name like Webber or Slotsky may not "sound" Latin – even though the writers may still be of Latin parentage or descent.

On Using Pen Names for Publication Bylines

On the fun side of pen names is the persona. They are often used in conjunction with our legal names, or not, as the case may be. When I was growing up, my parents had a friend who wrote a column for a North County paper under the name Luella Liverwurst!

Then there is Dr. Seuss, who locals knew was Theodore Dreisel. How did we know? Because our parents told us. . .Furthermore, he held workshops for kids of all ages at the La Jolla Museum of Contemporary Art. While I don't know how or why he came up with this pen name, it was, and continues to be, memorable.

On Using Pen Names for Writing Personas

Pen names are often bestowed upon us like titles in alien and ancient courts. When I was in graduate school, my department chair dubbed me "The Mistress of Rhetoric" due to my harping on how women received "Masters" degrees. . .A bit of feminist theoretical fun ensued (and no, I am not a militant feminist. . .). It stuck, and years later, I wrote a monthly column under the same name for San Diego's Cafe and Coffee House Scene, *The Espresso*.

In my capacity as a staff member at Sam's Dot Publishing, I often sign my name as The Boortean Ambassador to Haura. When our managing editor began addressing me by this title, it stuck. Over the years, I began to sign the *Drabble's* "A Note from your Editor" with such, and have even used it as a byline for my own drabbles and poetry.

As a scifaikujin, or writer of science and speculative fiction haiku, my haikujin, or haiku name, is semi. I have had quite a few traditional haiku as well as scifaiku penned under this name, which was bestowed upon me by my mentor. It means, "cicada", in Japanese, and has, of course, a special meaning given my association with a particular circle of poets.

Closing Thoughts

As long as your reasons for using pen names are not meant to break the law or otherwise escape justice, then my only advice is to choose wisely and be sure they're individually tailored. Who knows, you may just find, as numerologists will often claim, that your name is your destiny.

Writing for the Love

This piece was previously published online at suite101.com on October 18, 2010.

Many writers will "gift" their work to publications that pay in exposure-only. These are often referred to as "for the love" sites.

There are many reasons for beginning as well as experienced professional writers to submit their work to publications that pay in exposure only. In addition to the often-expressed gratitude, some of these publications actually "pay" with opportunities for reduced-price or "free" classified ads. Others offer contributor copies or other means of exchange. Yes, writers deserve to be paid for their work--and well. However, being paid may not be their primary motivation for writing.

Start-up Publications

When a publication first launches, they may be on a small budget or operating under a grant. The staff often works for free as well, as they are publishing said publication "for the love". Some publications may communicate that they hope to and/or plan to eventually pay their writers. A start-up publication is, after all, a start-up business. Once ads are sold, or other means of income are established, then they may change their status to a semi-pro or a pro standing.

Creating and Expanding a Writing Community

Established writers may choose to submit their work to a "for-the-love" publication in order to assist that publication in gaining a presence. They may also do so because they really like what the editors are doing or they are in what is usually termed, "good company". Perhaps they're championing a good cause, hosting a fund-raiser, or maybe there's just an unusual or fun theme. Regardless, word travels fast within writing communities both on and off-line.

Paying it Forward

Submitting work to an exposure-only site is also a great way to pay it forward, a way to thank an individual, a small collective, or the reading and writing community at large. If a writer has been mentored or encouraged by another more established writer (or editor), then submitting to a site in their circle is a way to show appreciation.

Since word travels nearly as fast as thought at internet watering holes, bulletin boards, and blogs, if a trusted writing acquaintance or friend urges others to consider submitting to a new, semi-established, or well-established zine that needs work, then that publication may often experience a barrage of submissions!

Creating a Writing Presence

Another reason for submitting to an exposure-only publication is that it's a way to create, maintain, or otherwise perpetuate your writing presence. Whether it's a nonfiction writer focused on building their "clip file", or published samples of their work, a fiction writer who wants to keep their name recognition out there while also focusing on a novel, or a poet crossing genres, it is not unusual for them to turn to "for the love" publications.

Academic Publications

Many academic publications or journals don't pay their writers. It's considered part of the professional life-style as well as essential for continued employment on the proverbial tenure-track. True, many academics are paid--and well--for journal articles, book reviews, and so forth, but there are still quite a few out there that invite submissions in order to share and discuss theory, practice, and other academic concerns. Knowledge, as the saying goes, is meant to be exchanged!

Closing Comments

Why do so many writers submit to "for-the-love" publications? Could it be that they, as well as the publications which offer "exposure-only", are doing it for the love of the reading and writing public? They have a story to tell, an experience to share, or are otherwise compelled to add their thoughts to an ongoing discussion.

While the purpose of this article is not to urge writers to give their writing away, it is to advocate for those who choose to do so - whatever their reason. The next time a publication states that they pay in exposure and gratitude only, consider the ramifications of those words. There may come a time when they are able to pay professional rates, and guess who they'll personally contact?

Searching for Freelance Writing Gigs: Websites for Freelancers

This piece was previously published online at suite101.com on September 8, 2010.

This is Part I of a series of articles on finding freelance and other types of writing assignments.

Since there are such a vast number of websites that advertise freelance writing assignments, it is often difficult to determine the ones that are best-suited to a writer's particular skill set and interest. The question of legitimacy may also arise, as will the quandary when deciding whether or not it is worthwhile to pay for access to certain sites. Then there are those sites that engage in "bidding wars" where many writers may seem to offer their services for a paltry sum in order to get the gig. The adage, "You get what you pay for," does not always apply to writers, as there are many professionals who will write "for the love" (i.e., "for free").

While many writers are just getting started or are willing to write for small stipends in order to create or expand their reputation and otherwise add to their credits, the field is still overflowing with more experienced writers who make, or exceed, a living wage. It's important not to become disheartened by real and/or imagined competition. As this writer was always cautioned: It takes persistence as well as talent to succeed.

An Overview of Sites for Freelance Writers

In addition to registering at obvious sites such as guru.com and monster.com, craigslist.org has world-wide listings for writers under "writing/editing", as well as under "gigs". Pay-per-click sites such as Suite101.com are common, as are sites that may pay a small advance for articles such as DemandStudios.com and AssociatedContent.com, but with some restrictions. Federal, state, county, and city government sites occasionally list positions which include interim as well as temporary positions for writers, but these positions usually call for grant writing as well as technical writing. Philanthropic organizations as well as NGOs, or non-government organizations, may often have calls for grant writers.

Additional Sites for Freelance Writers

Preditors & Editors, as its name implies, is a portal of resources for writers and editors. Available at pred-ed.com, their home page states that they are, "A guide to publishers and publishing services for serious writers since 1997." Their "Jobs" section provides an "A-Z" listing, which is regularly updated. At this writing, there were approximately thirty-five listings. One of the strong points about P&E is that they welcome and provide feedback.

While writers organizations such The Horror Writers Association, available at horror.org, and the Science Fiction & Fantasy Writers of America, available at sfwa.org, have membership criteria as well as dues, both organizations have bulletin boards and newsletters which include calls for fiction as well as non-fiction submissions. Organizations such as these provide invaluable mentorship as well as conferences and other social networking opportunities.

Ralan.com is a free market list that includes postings for a variety of genres and their respective publications. This site is not only for fiction writers and poets, as many publications which publish fiction, etc., will also be looking for articles on subject areas related to their genre as well as criticism.

Many author sites will also offer free newsletters complete with calls for submissions and contests. One such site is Horror Writer and Educator, Michael A. Arnzen's gorelets.com.

It's important for writers of any type to honestly assess their skill level, ability to make deadlines, as well as areas of interest and expertise when further honing their job search. Be sure to have an updated resume as well as a collection of clips, or writing samples, just in case the next position applied for requests them.

Q & A: There's no such thing as a Stoopid Question

According to David Boyne, the former publicist for writersmonthly.com and *WORD Magazine,* and the first human to give me a regular column spot in cyber space, this section was one of his readers' favorite stops at the site.

On Assonance and Consonance in Poetry

Assonance is the repetition of vowel sounds such as the long "ou" in "sound" and "down". It's not the same as a direct rhyme, which would occur with the pairing of "sound" with "found" or "hound".

Consonance is the repetition of consonant sounds such as the "b" in the following phrase "moon-burned blood". Alliteration is the repetition of consonants at the beginnings of words, such as the following: the burnished bronze of autumn leaves bore witness to summer's end."

On Free Verse

Free verse (also known as blank verse) is a poetic "form" that doesn't follow a "traditional" structure or scannable metric pattern (e.g., sonnets, rondeaus, etc.). According to **Mary Oliver** in A Poetry Handbook: ***A PROSE GUIDE TO UNDERSTANDING AND WRITING POETRY,*** Walt Whitman "is frequently cited as the first American poet to write in free verse" (San Diego: Harcourt Brace, 1994. 70.). Much of what we consider to be "modern" poetry—even experimental poetry—has elements of free verse.

Check out this Walt Whitman Hyperpoem Project: http://www.villarana.freeserve.co.uk/Walt.htm

On Suggested Reading—from Poet/Novelist Bruce Boston

This time I asked the question and received an excellent response—from Bruce Boston. Thank you Bruce…

Q: Do you have a list of suggested reading?

A: Here are the major anthologies in the field as I see them. Some of the details in the following list borrow, with thanks, from Steve Eng's excellent survey article on SF poetry that appears in Anatomy of Wonder 4 edited by Neil Barron (R. R. Bowker, 1995).

Holding Your Eight Hands: An Anthology of Science Fiction Verse, ed. by Edward Lucie-Smith, Doubleday, 1970. 58 poems by 36 poets, including Brian Aldiss, John Brunner, Thomas Disch, and C.S. Lewis.

The Umbral Anthology of Science Fiction Poetry, ed. by Steve Rasnic Tem, Umbral Press, 1982. 141 poems by 61 poets, including Ray Bradbury, Disch, Robert Frazier, and William Stafford.

Burning with a Vision: Poetry of Science and the Fantastic, ed. by Robert Frazier, Owlswick, 1984. 130 poems by 56 poets, including Michael Bishop, Ursula Le Guin, Jane Yolen, Bruce Boston, and Loren Eisley.

POLY: New Speculative Writing, ed. by Lee Ballentine, Ocean View Books, 1989. A mix of both fiction and poetry, with an emphasis on surrealism and experiment. 69 poems by 25 poets, including Bradbury, Disch, Diane Ackerman, John Oliver Simon, Frazier, Boston, Andrew Joron.

Whispering Words, ed. by David Bain, A/A Productions, 1998. http://www.geocities.com/Area51/Shadowlands/4464/
The only major genre poetry collection online. It also can be downloaded as a PDF file. Billed as "nearly 150 poems of the fantastic by the best mainstream and H/F/SF poets of the 1990s." Includes Michael Arnzen, Boston, Keith Allen Daniels, Corrine DeWinter, Frazier, John Grey, D. F. Lewis, Jacie Ragan, Darrell Schweitzer, W. Gregory Stewart, William John Watkins, t. winter-damon, and many others.

2001: A Science Fiction Poetry Anthology, ed. by Keith Allen Daniels, Anamnesis, 2001. 125 poems by many of the top contemporary poets in the field. Includes Boston, G. O. Clark, Frazier, Charlee Jacob, David Lunde, David Memmot, Wendy Rathbone, Ann K. Schwader, Steve Sneyd, Mary Turzillo, Watkins and others.

On Science Fiction Poetry

Let's begin with a short quiz.

Please choose your responses from the items listed.
1. Science Fiction poetry is based on hard science.
a) true b) false c) both true and not true d) both false and not false e) neither true nor not true or false nor not false f) all of the above g) none of the above h) this woman is definitely lunar i) what was the question? j) Next question, please! k) Where's Heidigger when you need him? l) Schroedinger's cat m) Is this "beam-me-up-Scotty-time"?

2. Science Fiction poetry has nothing at all to do with hard science, but is speculative in nature.
a) True b) True some of the time, but not all of the time c) False d) False some of the time, but not all of the time e) As with most SF greats (e.g., Asimov, Arthur C. Clarke, Bradbury, Vonnegut and all they spawned), SF poets are visionaries f) If William Shakespeare was alive today, he would be writing SF poetry

3.If studies show that there is a probability of intelligent life existing on earth, and if evidence of intelligent life can be observed and measured by the interrogative process, then list your questions below:

Aren't quizzes fun?! Since one of the more practical ways to learn about a poetic form, or genre, is to read examples of it. To get you started, I've provided a few links:

The Martian Wave, The Fifth Di..., and Aoife's Kiss (all available at: http://www.promartian.com) have poetry in every issue. If you cruise on over to the **Creator's Club**, you can also see the archived work of several SF poets, including Yours Truly. **The Science Fiction Poetry Association** (available at: http://dm.net/~bejay/sfpa.htm) has a newsletter, information about events, "who's-who", and other goodies as well. **Tom Brinck's Scifaiku** site (available at: http://www.scifaiku.com) was my original port of entry. Life hasn't been the same since I joined the scifaiku list. Let's just say I've folded time and space, journeyed to distant galaxies, and encountered numerous aliens. **"The Ultimate Science Fiction Poetry Guide"** (available at: http://www.magicdragon.com/UltimateSF/sfpo.html) will keep you busy for a millennium or two.

Writing Exercises:
Who needs a gym or a personal trainer when you can be your own writing coach?

Exercise 1

Make a chart of random words, then cut them out, put them in your writer's hat (or even a brown paper bag), then draw a few at a time for inspiration or a writer's challenge. This is fun to do with the proverbial me, myself, and I, as well as your writing friends. It's also a great way to start a party, to bond with others, and the list goes on and on and on. . .

Exercise 2

Do you like to write list poems? Need some questions to facilitate your process, to get you started? You can copy then cut these into strips, pass around a writing group, or use as an ideas list.

1. What do you find in a café?
2. What do you find at the mall?
3. What do you like about the beach?
4. What do you like about yourself?
5. What do you like about your lover?
6. What do you dislike about (fill in the blank)?
7. What do you see out the window?
8. What's in your purse? Your book bag?
9. What do you see in the room?
10. What do you see when (fill in the blank)?
11. What do you taste when (fill in the blank)?
12. What do you smell when (fill in the blank)?
13. What do you feel when (fill in the blank)?
14. What do you hear when (fill in the blank)?
15. What do you sense when (fill in the blank)?
16. When I first get up, I (see/feel/taste/hear/smell/touch, etc.)
17. When I go to bed at night, I (see/feel/taste/hear/smell/touch, etc.)
18. What do you do at work?
19. What do you do at play?
20. What do you do when you meditate/contemplate, etc.?
21. What do you make? Unmake?
22. Close your eyes, imagine a place, describe it.

23. What's in your mind/thoughts/feelings?
24. What parts of your body are you aware of now?
25. What type of energy are you sensing/feeling?
26. Stop, listen—what do you hear?
27. A day in the life of…
28. Winning lotto numbers
29. Books that you've read
30. Movies/films that you've watched
31. Poets/authors that you read
32. Music that you listen to
33. What's growing in your garden?
34. What's growing in your refrigerator
35. Describe your house or apt.
36. Describe your parents' or grandparents' home
37. Describe your car
38. What's in your closet?
39. What's on your desk?
40. Good luck charms
41. Favorite things to eat
42. What are your personal drivers?

Exercise 3

Design your own workout here. What are your writing goals? What challenges you the most? The least?

Exercise 4

Come on! It's time for multiple reps—and no cheating! Be sure to increase the weight, too.

Exercise 5

Have a writing "get-together." In addition to other essential goodies, have your guests bring prompts to share, then feast!

Exercise 6

Do you have a bibliography or your published works pulled together? If not, start it here. If so, use this space to list the publications within which you'd like to appear—and manifest it!

Exercise 7

Do something outrageous and write about it here! Share it with the universe in a poem, short story, article, blog, novel, or screenplay!

Exercise 8

Model one of your favorite writer's poetry or prose here.

Exercise 9

Create a list of your favorite websites and publications here—then make a submission chart!

Exercise 10

Stare at this blank space and see what emerges.

Exercise 11

Focus on this blank page, then draw, paint, or collage what you see. Go for a multi-media extravaganza and combine image and text!

Exercise 12

List who—and what—you're grateful for here. . .Then write about it in more detail.

Exercise 13

If you don't have a new stack of clay tablets, stone monoliths, wood logs, wall space, notebooks, journals, napkins, brown paper bags, or other materials, now's the time to go get some, as this is the last blank page. Fill this page with shopping lists (for your writing studio), floor plans (for your writing studio), architectural renderings (for your dream house where you will have a writing studio), as well as ideas for future poems, short stories, screen plays, novels, interviews, reviews, or articles!

Exercise 14

There are so many sites out there with contest themes. What? The ones that inspired you have expired? No worries, as we say in Ocean Beach. . .You don't have to enter the contest to try out that prompt. Here are just a few sites that post, or hold, thematic contests.

Many publications hold contests from time-to-time, so be sure to visit your favorite online or print publications and scour them through-and-through. I've included a few general submission markets in here that have archives with past prompts, accordingly. For contests that post their submissions, it's excellent practice to read archived and ongoing content

If you're already an avid contest submitter, and haven't already read the articles on scams at Preditors & Editors and elsewhere, be sure to read the Science Fiction & Fantasy Writer's "Writer Beware" article, "Contest and Award Fakes Is it Worth it? Assessing Contests and Awards" at sfwa.org.

AbsoluteWrite's Index of Flash Fiction Markets: Last verified on 29th April 2011.
http://absolutewrite.com/forums/showthread.php?t=59234

A Word with You Press: Publishers & Purveyors of Fine Stories
http://www.awordwithyoupress.com/

Dark Moon Digest
http://darkmoondigest.com/

Michael A. Arnzen's GORELETS
http://www.gorelets.com/

NPR's Three-Minute Fiction Contest
http://www.npr.org/series/105660765/three-minute-fiction

Ralan.com Ralan's SpecFic & Humor Webstravaganza
http://ralan.com/m.contest.htm

*Star*line, The Science Fiction Poetry Association*
http://www.sfpoetry.com/contests.html

The Bulwer –Lytton Fiction Contest
http://www.bulwer-lytton.com/

The First Line
http://www.thefirstline.com/index.htm

Writers Digest: Writer Better Get Published
http://www.writersdigest.com/competitions

Exercise 15

Here are some first lines from a few of my unpublished and published stories. . .See what you come up with, and if they're published, be sure to credit me accordingly! You could also send me a list of your first lines, and I'll hold a contest accordingly—or use it for a drabble them, or. . .

1. I was around eight years old when I first discovered it in my bedroom closet. [2]

2. Miki leaned against the cool shower tiles wondering how many Guinness she drank at Nhan's party the night before and why he wanted her at the office on Sunday-especially after a party. [3]

3. Yes, at a quarter to 4 I wake up from ragged cliffs and torrential downpours, to aliens knocking on my bedroom window.[4]

---

[2] From "The Time Machine", which was entered in one of the *A Word with You Press' contests,* "Your Childhood is Calling", archived.

[3] From "The Mission Statement", which I confess was rejected so many times I lost count. I am now inspired to revise and resubmit it thanks to composing this exercise. Thank you, dear reader!

[4] From ". . .is when they come to visit." This was submitted to Sixbrickpress.com's *Six Little Things* "Quarter of. . ."contest. It was rejected.

Exercise 16

Do a Round Robin with a friend or group of friends.

Exercise 17

Since you probably know how fond I am of odd numbers by now, why not pen an ode or otherwise praise them here?

Exercise 18

Write a letter to the editor. Go ahead, send it. I'll be waiting.

Exercise 19

Sozar! I bet you thought I was going to end on an even number to mix things up. So, this is where you can play the Dadaist cut-up text game. Basically, you cut and paste text here. Don't worry about whether it makes sense. Have fun. Transcend logic. Be surreal.

Check out this cool site, the *Cut-up Laboratory* http://www.cut-up-lab.com/

Exercise 20

Write a press release for your upcoming book. If your book is still in the works, or you haven't begun it yet, write a PR AS IF it is hot off the press and on its way to the bookshelves!

Exercise 21

Explore classic and futuristic plots—and all the realms between. Here's a chart to get you started.

That new gourmet restaurant serves unusual fare		Boy-meets-girl-meets-alien		Asteroids plummet to earth
	DNA test reveals aberrant gene		Cassini satellite feed reveals alien architecture	
First humans to visit Gliese 581 d		The Rapture did happen on May 21, 2011		They seemed like such a normal family
	Earthquake in Greek Islands reveals entrance to Atlantian archives		Wedding on Europa, honeymoon on Io	
Heroic quest through time machine			Ground-breaking ceremony unearths evidence	

Exercise 22

Write out your plot points here. Who are your characters? What do they want, need? How do they resolve their conflicts?

Exercise 23

Are you a character or plot-driven writer? Both? Neither? Don't know? Begin a new story, or revise an older one that refuses to finish itself. If it's character-driven, rewrite it from a plot-driven perspective and vice versa. It that doesn't work, analyze the story from all angles to see determine what works, what doesn't, etc.

Exercise 24

Have fun with words here. . .To get you started, check out this cool site: *Worlds Gone Wild at* http://wildwords.us/.

Exercise 25

Experiment with various styles of writing. For starters, compose a rhopalic sentence or two! This is the stuff of which poetry is made, and will also make your brain burn—but in a good way! Relish in the sensation of synapses firing! It occurs to me that these could also be composed in reverse. I wonder what the term is for a mirror rhopalic.

In "A.Word.A.Day" etymology section note, at wordsmith.org, Anu Garg writes that "A rhopalic verse or sentence is one that balloons -- where each word is a letter or a syllable longer."(para. 5)[5]

Here's are a few phrases to get you started. The first two increase letters, and the ensuing three increase syllables. The fifth one is also a rhopalic poem, not to be confused with a tritail.

---

[5] Garg, Anu. "A.Word.A. Day." *Wordsmith.org: the magic of words.* 4 May 2011. Web.

1. The pier shook. . .

2. Meteors streaked. . .

3. Insomnia discombobulates neuroscientific. . .

4. Minoan excavation undeniably. . .

5. Hauran refugees. . .Tyraelian prokaryotics. . ..verminophobia heterogeneity

Exercise 26

When you encounter a sentence with an intriguing style (whether you want to emulate it or not), write it here. Be sure to include the bibliographic information!

Bibliography

"Using Numerology to Create Character Names." *Suite101.* Suite101.com, 26 Nov. 2010. Web.

"Using Pen Names – Readers Respond." *Suite101.* Suite101.com, 2 Nov. 2010. Web.

"Memorable Characters Need Memorable Names." *Suite101.* Suite101.com, 21 Oct. 2010. Web.

"Writing for the Love." *Suite101.* Suite101.com, 18 Oct. 2010. Web.

"Why Use a Pen Name?" *Suite101.* Suite101.com, 7 Oct., 2010. Web.

"How to Create a Title for Your Story." *Suite101.* Suite101.com, 29 Sept. 2010. Web.

"How to Title a Poem." *Suite 101.* Suite101.com, 12 Sept. 2010. Web.

"Searching for Freelance Writing Gigs: Websites for Freelancers." *Suite101.* Suite101.com, 8 Sept. 2010. Web.

"How to Write an Authorial Bio." *Suite101.* Suite101.com, 4 Sept. 2010. Web.

"The Postmodern Horror Film." *Suite101.* Suite101.com, 30 Aug. 2010. Web.

"Writers and the Need for Copyrighting and Trademarking." *Suite101.* Suite101.com, 29 Aug. 2010. Web.

"Some Thoughts on Odd Numbers and Creative Expression." *Suite101.* Suite101.com, 27 Aug. 2010. Web.

"How to Exponentially Expand Your Vocabulary." *Suite101.* Suite101.com, 13 Aug. 2010. Web.

"Banned Books Week, September 2010." *Suite101.* Suite101.com, 4 Aug. 2010. Web.

"Poetic Forms – How to Write a Triolet." *Suite101.* Suite101.com, 23

May 2010. Web.

"On Writing the Confessional Story." *Suite101.* Suite101.com, 20 May 2010. Web.

"Organizational Tips and Time Saving Strategies for Writers." *Suite101.* Suite101.com, 2 May 2010. Web.

"How to Write a Found Poem." *Suite101.* Suite101.com, 26 April 26 2010. Web.

"Performance Poets – Taking Poetry From the Page to the Stage." *Suite101.* Suite101.com, 20 April 2010. Web.

"How to Write a Horror Cinquain." *Suite101.* Suite101.com, 25 March 2010. Web.

"Tools for Writers – Working With a Thesaurus." *Suite101.* Suite 101.com, 23 March 2010. Web.

"What Editors Want and More Publishing Tips." *Suite101.* Suite 101.com, 19 March 2010. Web.

"How to Let a Story Find its Own Point-of-View." *Suite101.* Suite101.com, 15 March 2010. Web.

"Enhance Writing Skills With Sentence Combining." *Suite101.* Suite101.com, 7 March 2010. Web.

"'That Child Will Be The Death of Me': On loving the Mommies of Horror." *Tales from the Moonlit Path. Moonlit-path.com, Mother's Day Issue* Archives. Web.

"True Confessions from one of Horror's Many Lovers." *Tales from the Moonlit Path.* Moonlit-path.com, Valentine's Day Issue Archive. Web.

"Scrawled in Bloody Ink." *Tales from the Moonlit Path.* Moonlitpath.com, First Issue. Web.

"Psst! Wanna know the secret of Getting Published?" *Writer Online Archive.* 19 April 2005. Web.

"Writers Block? Never!" *Writer Online Archive.* 22 Feb. 2005. Web.

"Looking for Some Writing Ideas? Why Not Write About the Body?" *Writer Online Archive.* 25 Jan. 2005. Web.

"Adopt "Beginner's Mind' when Writing." *Writer Online Archive.* 11 Jan. 2005. Web.

"Taking Stock: Ordered Chaos?" *Writer Online Archive.* 28 Dec. 2004. Web.

"The Kung Fu of Writing: How to situate yourself in a daily practice and work towards that black belt." Poet's Workshop. *Writers Monthly Archive.* 2004. Web.

"To Simsub, Or Not To Simsub? That Is The Question…" Poet's Workshop. *Writers Monthly Archive.* 2004. Web.

"This Landscape Called Flesh." Poet's Workshop. *Writers Monthly Archive.* 2004. Web.

"Don't Forget to Breathe: Some thoughts on horror writing." *Writer Online Archive.* 20 Oct. 2003. Web.

"To Punctuate or Not to Punctuate (Therein lies the Question Mark)." *Writer Online Archive.* 20 Sept. 2004. Web.

"What's a Pantoum?" *Writer Online Archive.* 10 Aug. 2004. Web.

"Plotting with Playdough." *Writer Online Archive.* 14 June 2004. Web.

"How to Write a Sestina." *Writer Online Archive.* 1 June 2004 . Web.

"Wanna See Something Really Scary?" *Writer Online Archive. Web.*

"Poems of Place." Poet's Workshop. *Writers Monthly Archive.* 2003. Web.

"Poems from the San Diego Fires." Poet's Workshop. *Writers Monthly* Archive. 2003. Web.

"How to Let a poem go." Poet's Workshop. *Writers Monthly* Archive. 2003. Web.

"How to get a poem started." Poet's Workshop. *Writers Monthly* Archive. 2003. Web.

"Figure Enhancement Anyone? On Honing the Writing Scalpel." Poet's Workshop. *Writers Monthly* Archive. 2003. Web.

"On Resurrecting Dead Poems." Poet's Workshop. *Writers Monthly Archive.* 2003. Web.

"Who Are You? Some Comments on Writing the Authorial Bio." Poet's Workshop. *Writers Monthly* Archive. 2003. Web.

"Defining Speculative Poetry? Let's Not…" Poet's Workshop. *Writers Monthly Archive.* 2003. Web.

"Welcome to the Multiverse: The Science Fiction Poetry Association." Poet's Workshop. *Writers Monthly* Archive. 2003. Web.

"Serendipity: On the Art of Finding Poetry in Everyday Life." Poet's Workshop. *Writers Monthly Archive.* 2003. Web.

"Poetry and the Politics of War." Poet's Workshop. *Writers Monthly Archive.* 2003. Web.

"Reflections on Birth, Death, and Poetry." Poet's Workshop. *Writers Monthly Archive.* 2003. Web.

"Wanna See Something Really Scary?" Poet's Workshop. *Writers Monthly Archive.* 2003. Web.

"Writing in the New Year." *Writer Online Archive.* 29 Dec. 2003. Web.

"Don't Forget to Breathe: Some Thoughts on Horror Writing." *Writer Online Archive.* 20 Nov. 2003. Web.

"What to do when the sites are loading." *Writer Online Archive.* 17 Nov. 2003. Web.

"How to Avoid Getting Stuck in AP Mode: 10 Easy Steps for Troubleshooting Avoidance and Procrastination." Writer Online Archive. 3 Nov. 2003. *Web.*

"Don't Forget to Save." *Writer Online Archive.* 8 Sept. 2003. Web.

"Encounters with the Supernatural?" *Writer Online Archive.* 28 July 2003. Web.

"How to Avoid Getting Stuck in AP Mode: 10 Easy Steps for Troubleshooting Avoidance and Procrastination." *Writer Online Archive.* 3 Nov. 2003. Web.

"Science Fiction/Speculative Ghazals?" *Scifaikuest.* Nov. 2003. Cedar Rapids: Sam's Dot Publishing, 19-21.

"Don't Forget to Save." *Writer Online Archive.* 8 Sept. 2003. Web.

"Nature Gone Wild: Morphing Animals into Monsters." *Alienskin Magazine Archive.* Aug. 2003. Web.

"Encounters with the Supernatural?" *Writer Online Archive.* 28 July 2003. Web.

"How to write a pantoum." *Absolutewrite Archive. Web.*

"To Punctuate or not to punctuate." *Absolutewrite Archive. Web.*

"How to Write a Sestina." Poet's Workshop. *Writers Monthly Archive.* 2002. Web.

"How to Write a Sonnet." Poet's Workshop. *Writers Monthly* Archive. 2002. Web.

"How to Write a List Poem in 10 Easy Steps." Poet's Workshop. *Writers Monthly Archive.* 2002. Web.

"On the Benefits of Workshopping." Poet's Workshop. *Writers Monthly* Archive. 2002. Web.

"How to Revise and Publish Your Poetry." Poet's Workshop. *Writers Monthly* Archive. 2002. Web.

"How to Write a Pantoum." Poet's Workshop. *Writers Monthly* Archive. 2002. Web.

"Ad Astra! Science Fiction and Speculative Poetry." Poet's Workshop. *Writers Monthly Archive.* 2002. Web.

"To Punctuate or Not to Punctuate (Therein Lies the Question Mark...)" Poet's Workshop. *Writers Monthly* Archive. 2002. Web.

"Inspiration 101: The Grocery Store." *Writer Online Archive.* 31 March 2001. Web.

www.ingramcontent.com/pod-product-compliance
Lightning Source LLC
LaVergne TN
LVHW050625100826
845148LV00011B/1736